Take A Look
Through These
GREEN EYES
A Journey of Healing & Restoration

Tiffany Wilson Robertson

ISBN: 978-1-955312-58-5

Printed in the United States of America

Story Corner Publishing & Consulting, Inc.
3810 Indian River Rd. Suite 13031
Chesapeake, VA 23325

Storycornerpublishing@yahoo.com
www.StoryCornerPublishing.com

❧ DEDICATION ❧

I dedicate this book to my Lord and Savior, Jesus Christ. Thank you for giving me a chance to get it right another day. Thanks for allowing me to share your grace, goodness, and love with all your people.

To Florine Winnegan Thompson (Flo-Jo) and Harriet Wilson (Nana). You both made a humongous difference in my life. Flo-Jo and Nana, I miss you both dearly. I love you, and I'm thankful for every moment I had with you.

To my daddy, Ray N. Wilson. Thank you for all the life lessons, love, and support you have imprinted in me. Your transition presently is the most devastating storm I've yet to encounter. There are no words to express how much I love and will miss you dearly! I will never forget when you kissed me on the forehead when I was younger and said, "Goodnight, sleep tight. I'll see you in the morning." Today I say, "Sleep tight."

✺ ACKNOWLEDGEMENTS ✺

Thanks:

To my children for being there in the midst of it all and seeing mama go through struggle, exhausting work, pain, hurt, illness, etc. I love you, Shane and Caden. No matter what, trust God first!

To my parents, I thank you for helping me through struggles in my journey. We have had ups and downs, but we have gotten through the worst. I needed that support before, during, and after, and you both were there. I love you both dearly. I am grateful for all you both have done for me. Rest well, Daddy. Momma, Keep living! You can do this because God is with you.

To my brother, thanks a million. I always thought our relationship was normal between siblings, but I found out that just wasn't true. I love you so much.

To my best friend/ sister, Stephanie, on December 4, 2014, God carried you away. That was one of the hardest things I have ever had to deal with mentally. You were my rock, girl. You may not be here physically, but you certainly had much to do with the person I am today. It is because of you that I gave my life to Christ and never looked back. A few days before you passed, you and I were talking. We promised one another that if anything were to happen that we would save a seat for the other one in heaven, just like we always did when we went someplace. So, I know my seat is there waiting for me. I will be there when it's my time to join you. I miss you so much every day. Still, I cry, and my heart morns so heavy. At the same time, I can hear you telling me, "Stop that crying, 'cause you ain't going nowhere yet!" I know you are still here. It is just not in the way I imagined. I will never forget every memory we shared.

To my grandparents & great-grandparents: Harvey and Pearl, Oscar Sr. and Florine, Novel, and Harriett, thank you for giving me a little of each of you. Somehow you imparted things that I needed, and I still use them today. R.I.P., and I love you guys!

To my community, I thank you for the help, prayers, and love you have shown me daily. Thanks again, and I love you all.

To my church family, Oak Grove Baptist Church and Fair Oaks Sunday School, thank you, thank you, and thank you just for being the family with heart and love. Thank you for being there when I was not even a member. You all showed my family and I emotional support through all the good and bad. We can laugh, talk, hug, and cry together, and I'm grateful.

Pastor Holloway, thanks for being that pastor that calls, shows up in times of need, prays, helps others, is dedicated to the call, and preaches the word of God straightforwardly. I genuinely love my church, my Pastor, Leslie L. Holloway, and Lady Holloway.

∞ PREFACE ∞

"If the world hates you, keep in mind that he hated me first. " John 15:18 NIV

It is utterly amazing how God works. He has a way of getting his point across, and eventually, we find ourselves doing what he wants us to do. No, God doesn't control us. He is a gentleman and will wait on us. For those who have no clue, let me be the first to tell you. God is very persistent because He knows what's best for us. Let me say this: When God wants you to do something, He will stalk you until you give in. I could not sleep or get through an entire day without Him reminding me of my assignment. I could not even go to the bathroom in peace without Him speaking to me. So, let me get into the how, what, why, where, and who.

This book came about after God gave me a scripture in a dream, along with some other information. That morning I woke up and grabbed my Bible to look up John 15:18, the scripture quoted above. I read it several times, and I kept asking myself, "why would He reveal this to me? Why would someone hate me?" I did not understand it at all. I started doing some research on the verse to see if I missed something. I read it in different bible translations and looked it up online. I even asked people their interpretation of the verse—still, no logical explanation of why God would give me the scripture in a dream.

I even prayed to God for clarification but received no answers. The saying goes, "God's timing is not our timing." I was troubled by this for some time. My spirit was unease because I knew that it was something important that He wanted me to know. He always gives me messages through my dreams to remember. Over the following four weeks, publishing companies were randomly calling me. I even crossed paths with multiple authors that told me about the process of writing their first book. I initially thought it was strange, but after meeting so many, I wondered if it was a sign. I then began receiving junk mail from publishing companies asking if I wanted to become an author. At the time, I was so confused because I had no work to print. I had not registered for any author writing classes or publishing information. I wasn't even sure why I was meeting so many authors and hearing stories about their books. It was all peculiar to me.

Some time ago, I joined a Christian group. We would discuss scriptures every week. During one of our group meetings, I met a Christian author. He gave us so much information about his book that it sparked my interest. I began to ask him questions about the process. The more we spoke, the more he was ministering to me. God was finally revealing the answers to my prayers through this man. Everything became noticeably clear to me after that conversation. I understood what God was telling me all along. He gave me the assignment to write my own book. I became afraid and overwhelmed with so many thoughts. I started questioning God out of fear.

I worried about those who would be upset or even hate me after I completed my book. I knew sharing my testimony would include others in a negative light. I did not choose this assignment. It chose me. Walking with the Lord is not an easy road. You will have to endure some complex things. God never promised life would be easy. Sometimes there will be challenging hills to climb and rough storms. The one vital thing to recognize is God is always with us. Each time we graduate from basic training, we become stronger mentally, emotionally, spiritually, and even physically. The key is not to give up but continue on your path until you complete the course.

TABLE OF CONTENTS

ꙮ INTRODUCTION ꙮ

Have you ever gone through situations that were so profound or unreal that you had a hard time speaking them to others? I'm sure you have because I have been there too many times to count. Most situations we go through are to create testimonies that will free others. You can not have a testimony without a test, and life is full of difficult trials! I have learned it's not so much about the test but how you overcome the obstacles involved. There is a lesson in every test. Can you forgive? Can you move forward? Do you get stuck? Do you become bitter? These are just a few questions to ask yourself. Tests are created to make you stronger so others can see that it is possible to make it through the storm. God assigns every test because He is sovereign and controls everything. Nothing catches Him by surprise. He wants to see if we can put into practice everything, He taught us.

"Take A Look Through These Green Eyes: A Journey of Healing & Restoration" is a collection of testimonies that I have experienced that made me stronger and more confident. These testimonies helped me to go deeper in prayer and to see God from a different perspective. I have released these testimonies to exemplify determination, faith, and strength. You, too, can get through anything with God by your side if you do not give up.

The purpose of this book is to help someone else that may be going through or has gone through and still dealing with the trauma of a situation. I want to let you know there is a way out. Yes, you read correctly. There is a way out, and you can be healed and made whole again. You are not alone because God is with you. I am an overcomer by the grace of God. If I made it out of darkness and God healed me, it can happen for you too.

CHAPTER 1

Dreams

Dreams are images, ideas, emotions, and sensations that usually occur involuntarily in our minds. At some point, I want to think that everyone has dreams of their future, such as who they will marry, how much money they will make, their dream wedding, etc. Unfortunately, life can destroy those dreams. Our decisions also play a significant role in how our lives turn out. Do not get it twisted; some things are thrown into the mix, making the cake bitter to the taste and, on top of that, come out flat!

As a little girl, I dreamed of becoming a model. I wanted to wear pretty dresses and heels to walk up and down the runway. That dream was short-lived. I later dreamed of becoming a nurse. I would see the nurses wearing white uniforms, stockings, and shoes going from room to room, helping people. I was utterly immersed in the idea of being a nurse and having the ability to help people get better. The thought of that made my stomach flip with such joy. Going to the doctor's office was exciting as long as I was not the patient. In the hospitals, the nurses would move in different directions but somehow knew what each other needed and when it was time to tend to the patients. It was cool to see the nurses gather at the station and discuss a patient in detail without the charts in front of them. They remembered their patient's every detail. They valued their job. I looked at them as having superpowers! In my opinion, nurses are the most intelligent people in the world, and I wanted to be one of them.

As a young child, the desire to become a nurse was heavy on my heart. I could not shake it even if I tried. I knew it would happen someday because it just had to be God's calling for my life. I always played nurse with my dolls and my poor God sisters. We pretended we were at a hospital, and I was the nurse, and they were my patients. They never complained; they just played along. We even had a wooden stretcher in the house. We also had a medical bag that always stayed stocked. At any given time, I was ready to fix something or someone. I am grateful to have such wonderful memories with my God sisters, and I thank them.

I had typical dreams such as my dream wedding and marriage, my dream car, a description of the house I wanted to live in, and the number of boys I would have (I never wanted daughters). God was working in my life even at an early age. I was never the smartest in school. I hated it with a passion. I couldn't learn and retain the material. I always stayed on punishment at home because I always had terrible grades on my report cards. All the other kids could go out and play, but I could not because I was too stupid to get good grades.

On report card day, I would become mentally and emotionally sick because I knew I would get physically disciplined by my dad. He showed no mercy. I would be too worried to eat; instead, I cried the entire day. The teachers would want to know why I was upset because I would not stop crying, but I could not tell them why. I dared not to say a word to anyone that would get my parents in trouble! Not only would that have been my ass, but I felt it would have been my life. During that time, I had extremely low self-esteem because of my bad grades. I thought that I always disappointed my parents. I could not talk to them because they were not into listening to a child.

The rules were:

> Do what I tell you!
>
> I bought you into this world. Therefore, I will take you out too.
>
> This is my house, and you will follow the rules.

Then there was my little brother. He was smart. He did not have to study at all and still got good grades. He always was able to go outside and play. It was not until I was older that I realized I was not stupid. I did not learn the way most people did. I was a hands-on learner, and in school, all the children are expected to learn the same way. By God's grace, I never had to repeat a grade. I graduated from high school at the age of 17. I had to attend summer school to keep up, but it was worth it. When I was in the 12th grade, I finally made the honor roll list! I was so proud of myself. I could not wait until my parents saw my report card then. My mom was overly excited. My dad looked at it and said, "well, it's about time." I was devastated by his response. I just wanted him to be proud of me just once. To this day, he does not know how his response affected my mind and emotions. That was one of those hurts that stuck with me.

My guidance counselor told me that I would never become a nurse because I did not have the grades. I could remember thinking to myself that I would make it. I will become a nurse no matter what the counselor says. I was not too fond of math, and good math scores are a requirement to become a nurse. My counselor focused on my math grades and stood firm in her opinion. She said, "tiffany, you have to be strong in math to become a nurse, and you just don't have those skills."

Despite those words, I was still determined to prove everybody wrong. I began to volunteer at medical centers to gain some knowledge and to get my name out there. I just knew I could be a great nurse. I had to go about it unusually, or so I thought. While watching TV one day, I saw a commercial for a business college. By this time, I had accepted a full-time position at a childcare center. I worked in the infant room. I evaluated my life and figured I had nothing to lose, so I called the college the next day. They wanted me to come in and meet with the medical assistant program coordinator. After work, I went, talked to them, and took the test they required to get in, which included some math.

Guess what! I passed!!! I started night classes that following week. Soon after, I graduated with honors!!! I worked full-time during the day and went to school full-time at night. I would stay up most of the night studying. I loved it because it was what I wanted to do. It was nothing for me to get 2 hours of sleep, get up, and go to work. I did it! The college would assist the students after graduation to find a job, but I already had one lined up and waiting for me. Glory to God! I had already put in my resignation papers with the childcare center. I was ready to start my new journey that everyone believed I would fail. I went through the classes with a breeze. Everything was hands-on, just how I needed it to be. There was one area I felt I was not that strong in, and that area was phlebotomy (drawing blood). I just was not comfortable with that skill. That was not okay for me, so I had to do something about it. I applied for another job at a medical center to gain more experience in the lab. I went to the interview with the mindset that I already had the job. I was determined to do better at drawing blood.

The interview began with all the typical questions. The interviewer was impressed with my resume. She asked me why I applied for the position. I told her I was not that confident with drawing blood. Phlebotomy was the one area that scared me. I wanted to feel comfortable as well as be good at it. At that point, she looked at me strangely and said, "you do know this job is for a lab assistant, which 90% of the job is drawing blood, right?" I answered, "yes, I do!" That was the reason I decided to apply for the job. I think, instead of running from my weakness, I would rather face my fear. I asked the interviewer for a chance to prove myself. I knew I would become more confident with drawing blood once I got more experience. I knew I would be an asset to the company. The interviewer replied, "Wow! That is a first. You are hired." I guess she was shocked about my honesty. I was excited to hear the words, "you are hired!"

I started the new job that following week. I worked the evening shift with a lab technician named Mr. John Black. He was an older black man, maybe in his 60's. John wore dress pants, a button-down shirt, brown leather tie-up shoes with thick rubber soles, and a white lab coat daily. He served in the military during his younger years. Mr. John retired and worked at the lab because he wanted something to keep him busy. Plus, he loved working in the lab. John was a very laid-back guy, and nothing got him excited. John would get the job done but on his time. Then and only then would they get the results. John was not much of a talker when I first came around. The first night he showed me around the lab. The next night John showed me how to run a test. On the third night, he showed me how to draw blood. On the fourth night, John sat in his chair, leaned back, and bowed his head. He told me to call him if I needed him, then he went to sleep.

Good thing I was young with a good, strong bladder because we would have had a problem. Your girl was scared!!! It was not long before someone came for me to run a blood test. Luckily, I catch on fast when it's hands-on. To my surprise, I was able to get the blood and send the results to the doctor within minutes. As I stood there in shock, breathing heavily, I heard a deep voice say, "you did incredibly well." Yup, John was watching me the entire time. From that day, John and I became the best of friends. He would always throw me out there and see what I would do. If I needed help, he would be there.

John's famous words to me were, "you can do it, baby girl. Just believe in yourself." I wanted John to stand beside me when I did something new, but he wouldn't. He would wave his left hand at me while giving instructions from across the lab as he did other things. He would not even look at me. Within one week, John had me drawing blood, running blood panels and counts, printing results, and reporting them. I was still nervous about drawing blood, but I knew John would not bail me out. Therefore, I had to get it together.

During my second week, one doctor came into the lab in a panic. "I have a 2-week-old baby that I need labs for, and I have tried everything but could not get any blood. I must have this done immediately because this child is extremely sick," said the worried doctor. I just knew John was going to run the labs because I was new, and I was not that good at drawing blood. So, I stepped back out of the way. The doctor looked at me and said, "I want you to draw the baby's blood for me!" My eyes got big, my heart skipped a beat, and I was about to say "no." Then John stepped up and said, "yes, sir. She will be right there."

The doctor walked out. I looked at John like he had lost his mind while he handed me all the supplies I needed to take the blood. He looked at me and said, "baby girl, you can do this. Just believe in yourself. Oh, yeah. It will help if you breathe!" Then he laughed. I did not think it was funny because I had a tiny baby's fate on my hands. I just had to pray. I took the supplies and went into the procedure room. The doctor and both parents were there. The mother was crying, and the father was looking over my shoulder. I had a tiny 2-week-old baby lying on the table waiting for me. This moment was clearly not the time to show fear. I had to show confidence no matter what thoughts ran through my mind. I put my gloves on, and I started looking for a vein.

The veins of a 2-week-old baby are as thin as an ink pen mark. I remembered John's encouraging words and continued to focus. I put on the tourniquet, cleaned the area, grabbed the butterfly needle, found my vein of choice, and went for it. I hit the vein on the first try. I got the sample! I could hear the relief in the room from the parents and doctor. The doctor told me I was fantastic, and he would like me to draw blood for all his patients. I smiled and cleaned up, then went back to the lab. I gave John the blood samples because I had to sit down for a minute. I thought I was going to pass out. My adrenaline was through the roof, but I was glad the mission was accomplished.

John looked at me and said, "you did a damn excellent job! I know excellent quality when I see it." He hugged me so tight that I thought he would never let me go. He was so proud that I could feel it, and it almost made me shed a tear. No one has ever been that proud of me, and for the first time, I could genuinely experience that. After I gathered myself, all fear left me. I was no longer afraid. I had the confidence I had been looking for a long time. Today, blood collection is my most vital skill!! Thank you sincerely, John Black, wherever you are. I genuinely love you for all you have done for me. I would love to hear from you again one day.

CHAPTER 2

Needs

A need is something essential. Needs are something that must be fulfilled in all our lives. I am blessed to have a family that supports me and is there for me when I am in need. God knew exactly who I needed in my life. On July 30, 1974, I was born to Ray and Hilda Wilson. These two love birds had just built their home and wasted no time starting a family. My mother found out she was pregnant, and they could not wait to welcome a beautiful baby into the world. They were so excited. My mother is a lovely dark skin woman with chestnut brown hair and brown eyes. My father is noticeably light skin, with dark black hair and brown eyes. Keep that in mind as I paint the picture for you from my mother's point of view.

"I had a wonderful pregnancy and craved garden-grown salads. I could not eat enough! I did not even have labor pains. I can remember all the horror stories about labor and delivery I heard. I was told how it hurt, but I did not go through any pain. When it was time to push, I did with ease. I felt some pressure but no pain. Then a baby girl was born," my mother explained. That baby girl was me.

Back then, after a baby was born, the doctor would do an examination, and then the nurse would take the baby away to the nursery to be cleaned up. Once everything was done, the nurse would return the baby to its mother. After I was born and cleaned, the nurse took me back to my mother. She was excited to see me and could not wait to hold me. Once she laid eyes on me, she called for the nurse to return, my mother explained. She told the nurse there had to be a mix-up because she did not have the correct baby. The nurse took the baby away and returned to my mother to check her armband, which had a serial number that matched mine. The nurse informed her that I was her baby and there was no mix-up because our numbers matched.

Imagine hearing this story from your mother. I had to ask her why on earth she felt I was the wrong baby. She explained to me that I was born so light that I looked white, and I had bright sky-blue eyes with blonde hair. My mother was confused by this because my features did not match hers or my father's. She wondered how I could have been the right baby. On top of that, I was the only baby with blue eyes in the nursery, which happened to be black.

By this time, my Grammy Flo-Jo entered the room, congratulating my mother and ready to see me for the first time. My mother told my grandma she believed there was a mistake because I didn't favor her or my father. Grandma looked at mama and told her to look at the baby. Mama looked at me and told my mom I was hers, and I looked just like Harriet Wilson (my dad's mother).

As for my daddy's point of view concerning my birth, he saw things a little differently. "It was time for Hilda to have the baby. I was scared and excited all at the same time. I tried to be as supportive as I could as her husband, but I did not want to see too much. Long story short, our baby girl was born, and I looked at her and thought she was ugly because she was so pale. Then when she opened her mouth, she had green stuff in there, which may have been the salad Hilda ate all the time," my dad explained with laughter. My dad said he left the delivery room to update our family in the waiting room.

I was so shocked to hear my parent's story of what they thought when I was born. It's not every day parents disown their child at birth. I wasn't sure what God had in mind when He made me, but this sista had a rocky start!

I think God thought my mama and daddy needed excitement in their life, so He sent them me for a child. I have kept them on their toes since birth, and I still do. Ha-ha! My mama and daddy gave me everything I needed. They even supplied some of my wants too. I have never been hungry, homeless, or without clothes and shoes. In fact, my mama kept my clothes ironed, folded neatly, or hung up. She would even iron my socks and underwear to fold flat in my drawers. The creases in my pants were so sharp and stiff I would wear them all day, and still no wrinkles! I would put on a pair of pants, and they would make noises when I walked because they were so crisp.

My mama made sure my hair was done every day. I had exceedingly long and thick hair. I was reminded of my mama's heavy hand and strength whenever she combed my hair. When she would do my hair in two ponytails, I often looked Chinese because my hair was so tight. I always had painful hair bumps around my hairline where the most tension was from the tight ponytails. It was like my skin was playing tug-of-war with my hair. I had to learn fast how to do my own hair. Hallelujah! Thank you, Jesus, for showing me quick hair techniques! I was still very blessed to have a mother willing to ensure I looked nice. In my youth, I was a very active "tomboy" that wanted to do the things most boys like doing. I wanted to play in the dirt, climb trees, play with bugs, etc. I loved the outdoors. My parents wanted me to be more girlie and wear dresses, put bows in my hair, and play with dolls. They did not want me to wear sneakers as much, but I desired the complete opposite.

I thought I kept them busy and was too much for them to handle. Apparently, I did not keep them busy enough because two years later, they had another baby. A boy named Timothy.

He was cute, and it was not so bad having him around. He looked like a normal kid and did not have the drama I had when I was born. He had a beautiful caramel complexion with semi-curly brown hair and brown eyes. I called him Timmie. Timmie and I grew up together, and we had a typical brother/sister relationship. One minute we were fighting, and the next minute we were playing. We had the best times together. Mama and daddy had always been able to supply us with our needs. God knew what He was doing when he planned our family. We both were blessed from day one. We were loved to the core by our parents.

As siblings, we were extremely close and still are present. Our parents never had to worry about us fighting over money, games, shoes, or other material things because we both wanted the other to be happy. Our parents did not have to worry about us because we watched out for one another. We played together as kids, and we partied hard together as teens. All that was written to make clear that we are not perfect nor rich, but in some ways, we are because we have love for each other. I value that above all things. Our parents instilled in us respect, love, support, and ambition. No matter what came our way, we knew how to handle ourselves. God knew what Timmie and I needed in our lives to help us be the vessels He wanted us to become. Our parents had us in church all the time, although I would fall asleep. God was still working on me, even in my dreams.

"Train up a child in the way he should go, and when he is old, he will not depart from it." (Proverbs 22:6)

I honor my parents for training my brother and me in the ways of God. I thank them for their hard work and dedication. They were there through it all. From heartache, tears, disappointments, fears, etc., I will never be able to thank them enough. That is just the beginning of pouring out my heart.

Another critical need was education. Having an education is fundamental to having any chance of having a decent life. We, as people of color, should take every opportunity to advance and educate ourselves. Society shows us that the more education you have, the more freedom there is available to you. Confidence and self-esteem are vital to having a solid backbone and mindset. Do not let anyone control you or your mind because it is a horrible place to get stuck. The more truth you know, the better off you will be in life. Timmie started young in learning his trade. He was about six or nine months old when he began learning exciting things. He was even able to sit up by himself fully. Our granddaddy (Gang-Gang) would prop Timmie up beside him in his pickup truck and take him for a ride.

Timmie was with Gang-Gang most of the time. By the time Timmie was walking, he could already get certain tools Gang-Gang had needed for certain projects. Granddaddy believed in teaching us how to fix things ourselves. He would tell me that just because I was a girl didn't mean I would stay in the house. He taught me how to work on cars as well. Granddaddy explained to me that women had to work harder and get paid less than a man in the real world. Therefore, I had to be prepared sooner than later.

My granddaddy taught my brother and me to drive at the age of seven and eight. We would drive to the store near the house to get him some cheese from Barlow's. There were no seat belts or car seat laws then, so the police never bothered us when we drove. Yes, there were driver's license laws, but that did not scare us because we were confident drivers.

Timmie and I would drive to the store and tell Mr. Parker Barlow grandaddy wanted some cheese. He would get a big round chunk of cheese wrapped in white paper and cut off a block. Mr. Barlow would then cover the cheese and give it to us so we could return home. Back then, people would charge items on an account for the customers. Therefore, we could go into the store with no money to get the items, and granddaddy would pay it off later. Of course, Timmie and I would not get things for ourselves on credit. Grammy (Flo-Jo) would give us money for candy, chips, or soda. Those were the days!

Granddaddy even took time with us to teach us how to shoot guns. He always told me to "shoot first and ask questions later." Because of my Granddaddy, I know how to do many things the typical woman would not do. I know how to change the oil in a car, how to change a tire, and how to identify the different parts of a motor. I have my own tool bag filled with lots of various tools. My granddaddy would say, "if it is broken, hell, you can't do no worst! At least try to figure it out." Grammy Flo-Jo showed me how to get work done no matter what and that working outdoors was necessary. "Dirt is good for ya," she'd say. My grandma was also a fast runner! She would run after Timmie often because he stayed in trouble. Grammy also taught me how to be a strong woman and never to give up. She was a tender, kind, loving, and no-nonsense grandmother. Flo-Jo and I spent a lot of time together. She was the first to know my secrets, problems, struggles, etc. One of her favorite sayings was, "it's cold out, so get on a jacket before you get the "Collie Molly" in your red ass." I'd ask, "what is the "Collie Molly"?" She'd say, "you will know when you get it!" I would be so confused but would think it was so funny. I really miss all the time we shared.

My grandparents were not the average grandparents. They had a small farm with chickens and hogs/pigs. We helped feed the pigs and get eggs out of the chicken coop. We stayed busy as children, but it never seemed like work because we had the best time learning new things. It was nothing like getting in the pig pen with all the mud to play with the baby pigs. They were fast, so we had to work hard to catch one. We would stay outside all day unless we got hurt or when it was time to eat. Gang-Gang and Grammy did not have a bathroom in their house. They had a wooden outhouse. So we did not have to go inside to use the bathroom. It smelled horrible in the summer, but that was a part of life. My grandparents had a large white pot with a thin red trim around the top that we used if it was severe weather, and the outhouse was not an option. The pot had a small missing piece on one side, so if you sat too long, there would be an imprint of "Pac-Man" on your hip. Ha-Ha! Some years later, they were blessed to have a bathroom installed inside of the house. I was blessed to have my grandparents in my life and even great-grandparents. I thank God for them all.

My great-grandparents taught me to garden in their old age. They even showed me that selling fruits and vegetables was a way to earn excellent money. My great-grandma, Ma Pearl, taught me how to crochet. She crocheted for years. She loved to crochet thin lace table mats and runners. I enjoyed it because it helped me to bring out my creative side. Ma Pearl would also tell me stories as we crocheted. One story that I recall was of her walking miles to school. To get there, she had to jump a fence and walk through woods and a field in all kinds of weather. One fence she had to jump enclosed a herd of cows and bulls. Ma Pearl said the big bulls would chase her every day, so she had to run really fast. She ran so fast that her body had difficulty keeping up with her feet, but she still made it to school. Other times she would tell me she could not make it to school because she had to work around the clock picking cotton. Ma Pearl even helped to plant and harvest vegetables in the garden. Ma Pearl was known for shelling butterbeans extremely fast because she had to shell them so much.

Nana showed me how to bake a cake and other sweets. She taught me how to cook, craft flowers and bows, etc. Nana also instructed me on what not to do, like, driving really fast, then slamming on the brakes. She would yell, "Shit! Do it all over again!" Nana taught me never to get dentures because I watched hers carry on a conversation while she was trying to speak at the same time. Ha-Ha! Those teeth never stayed in place! She even taught me how to be prissy. "Work them hips," Nana would say when I walked. I'm grateful for all the talks, secrets, and love Nana and I shared.

Great-granddaddy Harvey always threatened to cut my ear off so he could use it because he was 90% deaf. By the time I was done having a conversation with him, the whole community knew my business after I was done yelling loud enough for him to hear me. Granddaddy Harvey stayed in his trailer alone in his 90s and kept his gun close just in case he had to use it. Everyone in the community knew of my Granddaddy because he did not take any mess. They respected him and let him be in peace.

Ma Pearl also smoked a pipe. She had to have half and half Bacca, as she would call it. Ma Pearl could not smoke in the house, but she would do it anyway. If someone were to walk up on her, she would put the lit pipe in her house coat to conceal it. Grandaddy would catch her smoking all the time. He would walk into her room after smelling the smoke and ask Ma Pearl if she was smoking. Ma Pearl would always say, "Naw, Shorty." "Shorty" was my granddaddy's other nickname. As Ma Pearl denied smoking in the house, smoke would seep out of her pocket. It would be the funniest thing to watch. Grandaddy would always tell Ma Pearl to stop putting the lit pipe in her pocket before she set herself on fire one day.

My grandparents and great-grandparents are deceased now, but I appreciate all they taught my brother and me. They even met a lot of our needs. Of course, my parents had a hand in our development as well, but our grandparents and great-grandparents taught us priceless things we could never forget. They all imparted most of the things we needed to become who we are today.

I became an LPN in 2012 after nineteen years of being a medical assistant! I'm a real nurse now. Timothy (Timmie), my brother, went on to Aviation School. He is a rocket scientist, or at least that's what I call him. I am certainly proud of him. He can rip things apart and fix them as part of his job. I remember finding my dolls headless and his trucks broken up into pieces when we were younger. He would always manage to put his trucks back together again but forget about my dolls. As his sister, I would wonder why his head was so big. I guess his intelligent self just had a lot to think about then. Ha-Ha! I love you, Timmie. Again, God knew who all to place in my life, and I thank Him for it.

CHAPTER 3

Wants

Wants are desires to possess or something we lack but can do without them. We all have wants and, at times, think our wants or desires are as important as our needs. We can live without our wants being met, but our needs are necessary. Many people get so focused on themselves trying to fulfill their wants that they create a "Trump wall," which means sectioning themselves off because they think they are better than others. Our wants make us selfish thinkers at times. There are people in need every day. Instead of buying another pair of shoes, buy something for someone in need. We all know someone who has lost something or requires something they can not accomplish on their own. Most people have lost compassion for others, so the best thing we can do is care for and love one another. We do not have to search for needy people often because they are in our family, neighborhood, job, church, etc. Everyone may not have had the opportunity to get a decent education, an excellent job, or have found someone with a bit of money to buy them whatever they wanted.

I remember working with sick patients in the medical field. Every day helped me to understand that others are in greater need than myself and that life isn't as bad as I thought. I am not saying I'm not important, but someone is always going through a more challenging time. I realized the things I thought were a need were only a want. If I could go without the desire, then it never was a need. Looking at the patients I cared for daily made me see that life isn't just about myself but learning how to incorporate others. If we have it to give, we should provide it. God honors that because His word declares it's better to give than receive. I do not mean just money, either. You can give your time, a ride, a temporary space to live, food, the wisdom of God, encouragement, etc.

We have forgotten where we come from daily. Not all of us were born with a silver spoon in our mouths. One person may be blessed with more, but instead of sharing with the needy, they would give it to someone who has just as much as they do. I have witnessed people treat others with no respect, average workers are not paid their worth, and others get talked down to while trying to help. I'm not sure if it's just a black thing, but I see this occurring with us the most. Most families of other races help one another more, so I always question our mindset. Many people of different races that I know are quicker to help black people than we support our own kind, and I think that's sad. I am black, but I was raised among a mixture of races. I even have white friends I consider my sisters! We genuinely love each other regardless of color, creed, or race. I have compassion for all, but the change must start with us. I often wonder what happened to us as blacks that pushed us away from helping each other. Yes, I know slavery happened, but why didn't that bring us together even more? We also can make choices to become better than they taught us. Once we got "free," we forgot about each other and even started killing and competing. I pray it will stop, and we will have unity. We would get so much more done working together.

It is time for us to help and love one another better. Stop being so high and mighty, and do not be afraid to help others. The person may be across the street that needs you the most. Just take a look. We all have fallen on hard times or short on a bill or two. Most of us try to hide it because we want to keep up a particular image or are too afraid of what others think of us. No one wants to go through bad situations. Check on your family, friends, neighbors, etc., and try to be a good friend. If you could help someone, do it without telling the world to look good. Just do it and shut up! Help can be done in many ways. It does not have to be money all the time. It could be your time, a ride, a place to stay, encouraging words, prayer, clothing, food, etc. Some people may just need someone to listen so their minds can be reset. If someone opens up to you, keep the conversation confidential and do not share it with others. That would do more harm to the person already going through hard times trying to find a friend they could trust.

We are all God's children. Therefore, examine your heart, and hopefully, the Holy Spirit will convict you to see how selfish and greedy many of us get while trying to fulfill our desires. I was even surprised to see this type of selfishness in the church. Many say they do things for God, but it's just to gain personal gratification. God is not pleased when our heart posture is incorrect while working for Him because we steal His glory by focusing on the spotlight. The only one we should strive to hear "well done" from is God. Otherwise, we place ourselves as an idol for others to worship. Whatever you do for God will last because we were created to serve Him. Do away with selfish thinking. God's desires should be the ones we strive to meet.

The church must stop being hypocrites who teach and preach love and compassion but do not resemble the Body of Christ. Once we walk in love, our desires will change then the Holy Spirit can move in our lives. After we taste Him, our thirst will become a need for God alone. I think this will help us to shift from our wants to others' needs. Examine yourself. Be intentional about changing your ways. We must all live according to God's word and how He wants us to live. The Bible tells us to help the poor, widows, and orphans. Have you done this? Just something to keep in mind. God blesses us to be a blessing to others.

"Take six months to sweep around your own front door, and then take another six months to leave other folks alone!" I love that song. This song reminds me to work on myself. I want to please God, not people. In pleasing God, I know I must bless others and show the love of God. I have seen families turn on each other too many times to get ahead, and that is not the love of God. It takes a very mature person to apologize for mistakes they have made. Our mistakes help us to learn more about who we are and what God can do.

My grandmother, Florine Thompson, always told me it was nice to get what I wanted. At that time, I had no idea what she meant. Now I can look back and laugh because I know exactly what she means. Wants are just the cherry on top of the cake, but it is not needed for the cake to taste great. We have become so greedy that we never feel like we have enough. We compare ourselves to others, and if they have something we don't, we want that too. We become so wrapped up in what we want that we forget there is always someone with less than us. Most people want something or someone, but it may not be the right fit. We push past the stop signs because we must satisfy our desire, then we are miserable with our choice. We waste time and money in some way, and that could have been given to someone in need. God does not take joy in us wasting anything. Wants constantly change with our emotions, seasons, situations, etc., because we don't know what we want most times. It is time for us to be more grateful for what we have and allow God to guide us in understanding our needs.

CHAPTER 4

Satan

Satan comes to kill, steal, and destroy. Who is he? The craftiest creature God created. He is also a beautiful Arch angel covered in dazzling gems who led worship in heaven but got kicked out of heaven by God because of his pride. He was named Lucifer in heaven. Now he goes by the devil, the father of lies, the enemy, the fallen angel, the adversary, and Satan, just to name a few nicknames. No matter what you title him, he is trouble and hates us because we have a chance at heaven, and he doesn't anymore!

There are many ways Satan works through people. If we have not repented for our sins, need deliverance, or have not accepted Jesus Christ into our lives, we have open doors that will give unclean spirits access to us, including Satan. Regarding spirits, God is the only one who can save and protect us. Therefore, we must yield to God and be in right standing with Him. We must accept His son Jesus and keep His commands outlined in the Bible. As Christians, we must always wear the Armor of God according to scripture. His armor includes the following:

The helmet of salvation, the breastplate of righteousness, the shield of faith, the sword of the Spirit, the belt of truth, the sandals of peace, and God's word in our hearts. (Ephesians 6).

When we fall short, Satan waits for the moments we get stuck in sin. He intends to win our souls for his gain. Satan waits until we are at our weakest physically, mentally, emotionally, and spiritually to attack. Then he uses our fears, family, friends, etc., to tempt us to fall deeper into sin. He uses anything and anyone to his advantage.

Let me tell you a story of two people destroyed by Satan's plans. There was a man named Adam and a woman named Eve. They both attended their family's church, or "home church," as many would call it. One afternoon after service Adam walked up to Eve and spoke to her. Adam was nervous, but he knew he eventually wanted to take Eve out on a date. Eve was not looking for a man, but she did notice how well Adam dressed, and she liked the fact that he went to church. She even loved the way he smelled. Eve did not want to be rude, so she conversed with Adam. Adam sounded somewhat intelligent and didn't show signs of being like most men. Eve smiled as Adam charmed her and even asked for her number. Adam and Eve exchanged numbers, and Adam asked her out on a date. Eve agreed, and they arranged it.

She couldn't believe she was going out with a handsome man who loved going to church. Adam and Eve had no children. Therefore, that was another plus. Eve was in her early twenties, and Adam was in his early thirties. Therefore, the age difference was perfect. These things are rare to find with men, so she knew she was on to a great start. Over the days, Eve began to count down the day of their first date. She could not believe the week was taking so long to be over, or maybe she was just too excited.

Friday night finally arrived. Adam picked Eve up from her house at 6 pm. Eve wanted to know the details of the date, but Adam kept it secret because he wanted to surprise her. Eve was even more excited because Adam was intentional about going all out for their date. Eve felt special. Adam even had a nice car and played all the good jams on the radio. Some would refer to the jams as "oldies but goodies." Eve loved every moment of it.

There were clear skies, warm weather, and a connection that Eve did not feel in a long time. Eve was relaxed and felt comfortable and safe with Adam. They laughed and talked the entire ride. Before they knew it, they arrived at their destination. It was the ferry! Eve loved the water. They parked and walked by the water until the ferry was ready to board. There were a lot of people out that night. The ferry had arrived, and everyone began to board. Adam and Eve stood along the side of the ferry to feel the cool breeze and view the picture-perfect scenery of the water. So far, Adam and Eve were enjoying the date and each other. The conversation was pleasant and filled with lots of laughter.

The ferry docked, and Adam had a fancy dinner planned for Eve. Eve could not believe how well Adam had put everything together. They went into the restaurant, and Eve loved every minute of Adam's presence. She loved the restaurant too, but it was something about Adam that was growing on her. She had been on dates before, but this one felt different. This one felt right. This one felt like "the one!" Adam did not have to do much. Eve was already emotionally open and attentive to Adam's every move. As they sat in the restaurant, they gazed into each other's eyes and drove deeper into the conversation. Adam could not believe he was on a date with a woman from church, and she was terrific. He was happy he had the confidence to ask her on a date. He could not wait for their second date. Adam already began to plan it in his head. To their surprise, it was already 11 pm, and they had to head back to the ferry. Once on the ferry, Adam desired to be closer to Eve because their chemistry meshed so well.

All he could think about was how sexy her lips were, and he could not keep his eyes off them. Eve did not want the date to be over but looked forward to seeing Adam again. Eve knew Adam was also into her because he kept getting lost watching her lips move. It did not bother Eve because she had thoughts of kissing Adam. She did not know when kissing would be appropriate, but she was ready for that day. Meanwhile, Adam could not contain himself after a while. Therefore, he took the initiative and gently grabbed Eve by the waist, stepped in, and gave her a long passionate kiss. Everything in Adam told him it was the right time, so he went for it, and Adam was glad he did. It was the best kiss he had ever experienced! Eve was speechless and almost passed out. She could not believe her thoughts were happening, which was beyond what she could imagine. She started to blush and tried to contain herself as much as she could while fixing her hair and trying to keep her legs from wobbling. All Eve could say to herself was, "Damn! I'm in trouble now."

The ferry docked, and Eve knew it was time for her to get home before she gave in to the lust that grew inside. Adam and Eve were hot, bothered, and ready for the next. They got into Adam's car and were silent on the ride back to Eve's house. Eve was unsure of what to say after that explosive kiss. Adam was on a mission in his mind and wanted more of Eve. Eve tried to keep her legs steady as she thought about the kiss, but they continued to twitch as the lust took over her body. Adam soon approached Eve's home, but he did not want her to go. Eve felt the same way. Adam opened her door and walked her to the step. They kissed goodnight, and that was the start of their journey.

Adam needed to see Eve again, and Eve didn't want to be apart from Adam. They began to spend so much time together that it was second nature for them. They dated for seven years. Sure, they had some ups and downs, but they were inseparable. They grew more in love every day. One afternoon Adam took Eve out to a restaurant for a bite to eat. Eve wasn't that hungry, so she looked over the dessert menu. Adam went to the restroom and then picked up the dinner menu. Eve was still trying to decide which dessert she wanted, but Adam was up to something else. Eve finally looked away from the menu because she could feel Adam staring at her. When she looked at Adam, he was holding a beautiful diamond ring. She couldn't believe it! She gassed for air and tried not to faint. Everyone around them had already noticed, and they were waiting for him to pop the question. He got down on one knee and asked Eve if she would be his wife. Eve was shocked, with tears running down her face. She was completely caught off guard because she was not expecting Adam to arrange a proposal. Eve said, "Yes!" She loved Adam and wanted to spend the rest of her life with him. Everyone in the restaurant stood up, cheering and clapping. They were excited about Adam and Eve's next chapter of life, marriage.

Eve planned the wedding from beginning to end and enjoyed every moment. On May 15, 1999, at noon, Adam and Eve were married. Eve felt like the happiest woman alive! They went on their honeymoon smiling from ear to ear the entire time. Although they could not believe they were married, Adam knew he had made the best decision of his life. He loved everything about Eve and never wanted to be apart from her. After they returned from their honeymoon, Eve packed her things and moved in with Adam. She was nervous because she had never lived with a man. Adam assured her that what was his was hers and wanted her to feel welcomed into their new home. They had so many wedding gifts to sort through that it took months to open them all.

After Eve finally got settled into the house, she could not look her dad in the face whenever she saw him because she thought he would look at her differently. Everyone knows what goes down in the marriage bedroom. So, Eve was embarrassed to think that her dad was picturing her and Adam in that light. Adam felt the same way about his parents. Eve held her head down around her dad for a while until she eventually got over the thoughts. One night Eve tossed and turned next to Adam in bed as they slept. Eve could not sleep for some reason, then jumped up after she realized she had peed on herself. Eve started freaking out because she could not believe what had happened. Adam woke up and tried to comfort Eve, asking her what was wrong. He did not realize she had peed the bed but saw she was freaking out and so upset. Eve calmed down and told Adam it was nothing. By then, it was time for Adam to get ready for work, so he went to take a shower. Eve quickly snatched the sheets off the bed and threw them in the washer. After Adam left for work, Eve cleaned the mattress and put new sheets on the bed. Eve immediately got dressed and went to the doctor.

Eve told the doctor what happened, and then he laughed because she was so hysterical. The doctor told her to calm down because it was normal. He assured Eve that he treated new brides who had never lived with a man. He told her it could be a stressful transition and that this transition in her life was a big deal. He also told her to give it time before she could feel totally comfortable. Eve took the doctor's advice and took it one day at a time. Eve did have an accident once more, but after that, she felt settled, and it did not happen again. She was even able to give her dad eye contact again two months after she got married. Eve picked up hobbies in her spare time that sparked her interest. Some hobbies were writing and creating stationery sets with matching envelopes. Eve loved to write, so she started sending letters to everyone. She was thrilled for them to see her new stationery designs. Adam commended Eve on her creations and told her he was proud of her. Eve felt empowered and loved her product even more. One day Eve gave Adam a letter to send off in the mail because she was in a hurry. Adam took the note with no problem.

Two weeks later, while Eve was doing the laundry, she noticed her letter in Adam's work bag, or so she thought. When Eve picked up the letter, she saw it was one of her stationary envelope designs, but it had Adam's handwriting. The envelope was still sealed shut and addressed to someone in California. Adam used one of Eve's envelopes with hearts to write this person. Therefore, Eve knew it could not have been for a man, but Eve did not know anyone in California. She did not think Adam did either because he never mentioned them. Eve put the letter back into Adam's work bag and walked away in confusion. Before she left the laundry room, something told her to go back and read the letter, so she did. When Eve opened the letter, rage took over, and she felt like she had a heart attack. She could not believe what she was reading as she stood in shock. Adam met a woman in California and had lots of feelings for her. He expressed how much he was into her and wanted to be inside of her. Eve was unsure how Adam had met the woman or if they had sex yet, but Eve was at a loss for words. Adam and Eve had only been married for two months, and Eve had just started adapting to the transition of living with Adam. Eve could not stop the tears streaming down her eyes as she thought their marriage was over. Eve had so many questions swimming in her mind.

Eve sat for a while trying to make sense of it all, then she called Adam into the laundry room and asked him to explain. Adam looked at Eve, puzzled until he saw the envelope in her hand. Adam knew there was nothing to say to Eve to cover up his mess, so Adam begged her for forgiveness. He dropped to his knees and told Eve it was just letters and nothing else had happened. Adam expressed to Eve how much he loved her and did not want to lose her. Adam told Eve he was a stupid and selfish man and that it would not happen again. Eve's heart broke because she did not want to believe the letter was true. Eve could not get any more words out of her mouth, so she grabbed her keys, jumped in the car, and left. She drove and tried to clear her mind, but tears poured like a flood out of her eyes, causing her to pull over multiple times. Eventually, Eve went to her parent's house and vented to her mom and dad. She did not want to break the news to them, but she had no one else. Eve needed to vent, or she would have exploded!

Although they were disappointed, they focused on encouraging Eve not to beat herself up. Eve could not understand why her husband would entertain another woman. Eve thought she did everything right as a wife for Adam, like cooking, cleaning, sex daily, encouragement, support, etc., but he still went to another woman. Eve wanted to know how she would trust Adam again after the situation. Eve left her parents and went to the beach. Eve knew she would find more comfort near the water. Maybe she would even get answers on what to do next. Eve looked out over the water the entire night and did not sleep. She watched the beautiful sunrise at the beach and felt a little refreshed but still tired. She called out of work and waited for Adam to leave the house before she went home. Eve needed time to get herself and her thoughts together. Adam tried to get through to Eve all that day by phone, but she did not answer. She was not ready to face Adam. Since Adam had to work late, Eve had much time to herself. By the time Adam got home, Eve was fast asleep, so he did not bother her.

The next day Eve was open for a conversation with Adam. She knew he would not drop the situation because he was in the wrong. Eve figured she would get it over with sooner than later. Eve still did not know what to say to him, so she hoped that he would help her to make it all make sense. Adam admitted that it was a dumb stunt that he pulled, and it wouldn't happen again. Eve felt she had no choice but to forgive Adam and move on because they were married. She forgave him but could not get that day out of her head. About nine months passed, and their marriage was drama and stress-free! Eve was happy because she took that time to start her healing process. One day Eve started to notice bills piling up and not getting paid. She knew Adam always paid the bills, and he did not report any problems to her. Therefore, Eve could not figure out why so many bills were lying around the house. Eve asked Adam if she needed to work more hours to help with the bills, but Adam told her everything was okay. He told Eve he had a lot on his mind, and some unexpected bills were added to his list, but he would pay for everything. Eve assured Adam that if he needed help, she could assist with whatever was needed. Adam insisted that Eve keep her money and be responsible for her bills, and he would pay his. Eve did not like that concept within a marriage because she took from it that "her money is her money" and "his money is his money." Eve thought marriage should be joint everything, including money. She wanted joint bank accounts, but Adam disagreed. Eve even noticed that Adam would hide the phone bill and his credit card statements. Adam would tell her she could see the light bill but nothing else. Eve thought it was strange, but she did not want any problems. Therefore, Eve left the subject alone.

Eventually, their marriage started to change, and Eve was not happy. She noticed how distant and sneaky Adam had become. Eve wondered if Adam was cheating again. Adam would even come home with an attitude most days. He turned angry and was always yelling. He never wanted to talk about his problems but bottled them all inside. Eve cringed whenever she heard his truck pull up in the driveway because she never knew what to expect from him. Adam and Eve did not hang out anymore or go on dates. Adam always wanted to stay home if he was not at work. Even when they attended family functions, Adam wanted to rush home, leaving Eve to get a ride from family because she was not ready to go. Adam did not like when Eve wished to stay behind. He knew the family always had something to say, and he was not trying to hear anyone's mouth. He wanted to go home, and that was that. Adam's attitude always upset Eve, but she kept it to herself. She did not want to start an argument.

It had been two years now since Adam and Eve got married. Their marriage problems had died down because Eve was determined to sweep everything small under the rug. She felt if it weren't a big problem, she would not worry about it as much. They had been trying to have a baby with no luck. Eve thought maybe she had to unwind from all the stress, and they would have a better chance. Eve thought if they had a baby, it would help their marriage become the marriage it was always supposed to be. Adam was on board with the thought of making a son, so they tried and tried. Eve got frustrated and went to the doctor to see what was happening. She did not think it should take that long unless there was a problem. After examining Eve, the doctor told her that her fallopian tubes had been sewn to her intestines. Apparently, at the age of five, when she underwent surgery to get a hernia repair, they accidentally messed up the procedure. That was the reason Eve was unable to conceive a baby. Eve decided to get the problem corrected so they could have a baby. In October 2000, she had surgery, and everything turned out well. On December 31, 2000, Eve found out she was pregnant and could not wait to tell Adam. They were happy, and Eve had hope again for her marriage. September 6, 2001, at 8:56 am, Eve gave birth to an 8lbs 7½oz baby boy. Adam and Eve could not believe they were parents. They managed to work together to care for the baby without killing him. Eve just knew this was the fresh start they needed.

Eve stayed out of work for six weeks to recover and to spend time with the baby. Eve did not want her bonding time to end, but she had to return to work. While sitting at work every day, Eve knew she would rather be home with the baby, so she talked with Adam. She wanted to know if Adam was okay with her staying home with the baby versus going to work. She did not want to put too much on Adam. Therefore, if he could not manage the bills alone, she would continue to work until the time was right. Adam wanted to make Eve happy, so he agreed. Plus, Adam knew he had made enough money to cover all the bills. Eve was so excited and went to work the next day to put in her two weeks' notice. Before they could blink an eye, the baby was nine months old and walking. At ten months old, the baby was talking and climbing out of the crib. Potty training and weening the baby from breastfeeding was even a breeze at eighteen months. Adam and Eve had a beautiful baby boy together. Eve was still in shock!

Once the baby turned one year old, Adam became controlling towards Eve. He did not want Eve to go anywhere or talk to anyone. Otherwise, it made Adam get angry. Eve was not sure what happened because she thought they were making progress toward a great marriage with their new baby. Adam would get so mad at Eve that he would punch the walls. Eve would look around the house and notice cracked paint and holes everywhere. She was alarmed but did not say anything. One day Adam got angry at Eve again and punched a hole in his closet wall, which made his clothing rack fall on top of him. Adam came out of the closet fighting his clothes, and Eve looked at him in confusion. Adam was under a lot of stress and grew bitter but did not want to release his worries to Eve. Adam began to abuse Eve verbally. That was the only way he thought he could get his point across. Adam would say things to Eve, such as, "I'm stuck taking care of you because you are not working. You are fat now and need to lose weight. You should do more around the house instead of sitting around, etc." He even told Eve to clean his closet by the time he got in from work, or there would be consequences.

Eve did not say a word, although she was hurt. She could not believe Adam was feeling this way the whole time. Eve thought they were in a good place, but the old Adam showed up with a worse attitude. She picked the clothes up and reorganized his closet. Eve even did more around the house to please him, but he was still angry. Eve did not know how else to please Adam, so she worried their marriage would end after fighting so hard to have a baby. She did not want to be the reason their relationship was over. Although Eve thought she had done enough, she had no problem doing more. Adam grew distant again, while Eve became depressed, sad, and lonely. Eve tried not to shut down, but it was hard. Eve figured Adam was not attracted to her anymore, so she would get dressed, do her hair, and put on a little nude makeup to walk around the house. If she went anywhere, she would rush back home because she did not want to make Adam upset. Eve would even call Adam on the phone while she was out to check in with him. If he was pleasant on the phone, she could calm down from all the worrying she did, but if he had an attitude, she knew to rush home even quicker. Most times, Adam had an attitude, so her time running errands were limited.

If Adam and Eve went to family functions, Eve had to sit with a smile and pretend that everything was great. Eve hated it because she was miserable and started to resent marrying Adam. She knew her marriage was far from perfect but desired to someday make it perfect. For marriage to work, Eve knew it would take both of them working together. Eve did not think Adam wanted that anymore. Therefore, she questioned their marriage every day. She believed Adam just married her because it was something nice to do after seven years of dating. Eve also wondered if Adam even loved her anymore or if it was just sex for him.

On top of everything going on, strange things began to happen. A man came to the door one day and gave Eve a letter. He told her their home would be auctioned off in two weeks because the mortgage had not been paid. Eve was so devastated that she dropped to the floor. The man left after putting a "sale" sign in the front yard. Immediately Eve called Adam and told him what happened. Adam was at work and told Eve not to worry because it was a mistake. Adam told her they must have had the wrong person, and he would take care of it. By this time, Eve wasn't at all convinced. The paperwork she held had Adam's name, address, etc. There was a phone number on the paper, so Eve called to try to find out what was going on. Eve was told that the mortgage had not been paid in months, and it was no mistake. Later that day, Adam came home and took the letter from Eve, and she never saw it again. The auction date went by, but there was no auction. Eve was relieved that Adam took care of the situation. To this day, Eve still doesn't know what happened. Eve never saw another letter again or any mail at all. Adam would rush home every day to get the mail so Eve would not read another note.

One day Eve got to the mail before Adam and ran across some ads that were addressed to Adam. They were advertisements for sex, phone sex, and porn magazines, which had all types of naked women all over them. Eve was shocked and could not understand why those things were being sent to Adam in the mail. She threw it all away, thinking it was a mistake and did not think twice. Adam got home and slammed the door open, yelling at Eve and questioning her about the mail. Adam asked Eve did she get the mail, and she confirmed she did with a puzzled look on her face. Adam told her to hand over the mail, but Eve told Adam it was only a bunch of sex stuff she threw in the trash. Adam got furious and yelled at Eve to retrieve the mail and demanded that she never touch it again. Adam told Eve since she was not working or paying any bills, she had no reason to bother the mail. Eve stood in complete shock. She had a bad feeling about all that transpired just because of the mail. Adam always told Eve that he made enough at his job for her to stay home and even convinced her to be a stay-at-home mother. Therefore, Eve did not understand the problem with handling the mail. Eve was done with Adam's attitude and wanted to find out the root of the shift in his behavior.

The next day Eve called her friend in Georgia to explain what was happening. The first thing her friend asked was, did she check the computer? Eve did not think to check it because she didn't know what to look for on the computer. Her friend walked her through the steps of checking the computer for any clues. By the end of the day, Eve had discovered over 300 porn websites that her husband had visited. Eve understood why so much money was being spent on the phone bill. Adam had a list of 800 numbers that he had been calling, but they were not free. He even had a VIP card hidden in his car to purchase XXX porn videos. Adam's patterns begin to stand out to Eve. On Sundays, Eve would go to church, but Adam stopped going and wanted to stay home. Eve wondered why he did not want to go anymore, but he brushed her off. One Sunday, Eve decided not to go straight to church, but instead, she left the house as if she did go, then drove around the block and waited a little while. She then went back to the house and popped up on Adam. To her surprise, Adam was watching porn while masturbating. He tried to get himself together as fast as possible while turning off the t.v., but Eve had already caught him. Eve was disgusted at what she saw and walked out of the house to go to church this time. After church, Eve's mind was made up to leave Adam. She packed her and the baby's things and then left the house. She stayed with her parents until she was able to figure things out.

Adam called Eve every day and even went to her parent's house to tell her how sorry he was and how much he loved her. Adam begged Eve to come back home multiple times. Eve loved Adam and wanted to give him another chance, so she believed him, packed her things, and drove back home. Adam met Eve at the door. He was relieved to see her and the baby again. He welcomed her in, then snatched her bags from her hand and threw them to the floor. Adam looked at Eve, and his eyes lit up with rage. He began yelling at her to pick up her things and get them out of his sight. Adam was angry at Eve for leaving him, forcing him to beg for her back. He told Eve she was foolish for leaving and even more foolish for returning. Eve realized Adam did not change. He got worse instead! Adam only said those nice things to get Eve back into the house to trap her from ever leaving again. Eve laid the baby down and picked up her stuff with tears running down her face. Later that night, Adam told Eve she better not try to leave again, or she would be sorry. He told her if he couldn't have her, no one could. Eve knew what that meant, and she knew Adam was serious about it. Adam physically abused Eve in the past, so she knew what he was capable of after that.

Physical abuse soon became a regular part of their marriage. Adam exploded with anger more often and controlled everything Eve did. Adam was afraid that Eve would leave him again, so he tried to scare her and watch over her as much as possible. When Adam was ready for bed, he told Eve she had to go as well. Adam would turn the TV off and signal her to get into bed. If she took too long to get to bed, he would pull her into the room by her hair. Eve was terrified and wanted to comply because she thought of their son. She was unsure if Adam would kill her, but she did not want to take any chances. She knew their son needed her in his life. Eve reached out to his mother for advice because she knew she couldn't talk to her family. Adam's mother would tell Eve to hang in there and blow her off with the "you know how men are" line. His mom did not want to get involved in their marriage issues, so she reframed from giving her input. Eve felt stuck and did not know what else to do. After a while, Eve became numb to the abuse and pain and went through the motions to please Adam.

Eve cooked four-course dinners for Adam to have his plate ready once he got home from work. When Adam had a bad day, he would often not eat. He would throw his plate of food against the wall and yell at Eve to eat it from the floor. Eve did not want to eat the food, but she did not want to make Adam more furious. Therefore, she picked the food up immediately and pretended to eat it until Adam walked out of the kitchen. Eve began to hate Adam. She was so sick of the way Adam treated her. Eve's nerves got the best of her from all the stress. She went to the doctor because she was not feeling well and found out they were expecting another child. Eve cried because she did not want another child with her abusive husband. She did not want to remember all the times Adam forced her to have sex with him. She knew she could not speak out against him because rape was hard to prove in a marriage. Eve had no idea that he had gotten her pregnant again. She was so depressed and felt dead mentally and emotionally. Eve was in a dark place and could not get out. She was unsure if she could escape from her husband with two children and survive. Eve contemplated getting an abortion, but she knew that was not the will of God for her life.

Eve questioned God because He was quiet toward her situation. She did not understand why God allowed all these things to happen to her. She thought she did everything right. She did not shack up but waited until she married before they lived together. She did not have children before marriage either. She felt she was a good wife and mother, but nothing was good enough for Adam. She felt so alone and wanted to give it all up. She wanted the pain to stop and even contemplated taking her own life, but she did not want to leave their son in Adam's hands. Eve tried to keep busy by putting up drywall and new closet doors in their son's room. She painted the room with fresh paint and put a crib together for the new baby by herself. Before they knew it, Eve gave birth to their second son on May 2, 2004. She had difficulty connecting with her beautiful baby because of all the trauma she faced from Adam. She fell into depression, and her grandmother had to stay a while to help her. Eve eventually managed to deal with all the hurt and pain alone. Their son had grown so fast that Eve could not believe the time had passed. Eve knew God had her in his hands, but she still felt alone.

July 4, 2006, Eve decided to take the kids to see fireworks. Eve's mom wanted to join them and asked to drive. Adam did not want to go because Eve's mom would be there, and he tried to avoid her. Adam told Eve that she and the boys could not go either. Eve continued to put the boys in her mom's car, ignoring Adam. As Eve walked around the other side of the vehicle to get in, Adam yelled at Eve and told her that he would take the boys away from her and she would never see them again if she got into the car. Eve got out and did not take the boys to see the fireworks that year. At that moment, Eve seemed to have come to her senses. She had enough and began to pray to God for a strategy to get away. Eve told her parents that she needed to move out in secret. Eve was unsure how to do it, but she knew she had no choice. Her marriage was killing her, and it was not a good example for their children. Eve was on a mission, so she went out and got a part-time job to start the process of moving out. She looked for apartments, and when Adam wasn't home, she would pack little by little.

Eve had not been this determined in a long time, but after Adam threatened to take the kids, she had to go all the way with her plans. She found an apartment she liked, so she met with the landlord, and they were willing to show her the place. Eve thought it was perfect in person. Therefore, she paid the deposit, and the landlord handed her the keys. Eve was so excited to finally be doing something for herself again and staying on track with her plan. She then went to the local police to make them aware of her current situation so that if any friction were to happen as she walked out of the house, they would be familiar. Eve was afraid for her life and her sons, but she loved her children so much that if she did not do it for her, she had to do it for them. Looking at her children gave her the strength to stick to the plan.

On September 2, 2006, the police escorted Eve out of the house so she could remove all her things and the children's belongings in peace. She did not want any problems from Adam. Eve's family even showed up to help her as well. They helped her take stuff from the house and drive it to her new place. After

Eve walked out of the house that day, she never looked back. Although Eve was physically free, she was not mentally free, and she knew it would take some time. She had to get through the trauma of suffering from mental, emotional, sexual, and physical abuse. She had to figure out where to start her healing journey. Moving into the apartment and unpacking was a breeze for Eve. She was excited. In no time, everything was put into its proper place, and it appeared as if Eve and the boys lived there for months. Eve's family even helped her with anything extra she needed for her new apartment. Eve was relieved to get away from her husband, but she still felt uneasy that Adam would find her. Eve was so unsettled in the new place that she slept on the floor at the front door for a month because she was determined to keep her children safe.

The local police came by her apartment often to check on her, and they would even call to make sure she was okay. Eve and the police had a special password so that if something happened to her, they would know she was in trouble. As the days went on, Eve grew stronger. Eve continued to work her part-time job, but it was not enough money to cover all the bills each month. Adam would only give her $20 to $100 for the children if he felt it was necessary. Otherwise, Eve was on her own. She decided to go to social services for help, and they directed her to apply for child support. Eve had never needed to ask for state assistance, but she was happy they were there to help.

Eve was able to get approved for assistance from the state and even received food stamps so she could provide more food for her children. She was so happy to have some burdens lifted off her that she could not wait to go food shopping. One day, Eve got called into the social service office because a fraud investigator wanted to investigate her case. The investigator told her that Adam expressed he gave her more money than she reported on her application. Eve demanded that her social worker show up for the meeting. Eve knew she had been honest and used integrity the whole time. The social worker joined the meeting and claimed she had no remembrance of the information Eve submitted. Eve figured the social worker was lying to save her job because she did not make a note of all the times Eve called to report the money. Eve was more upset that Adam would report her to interfere with feeding their children. Eve knew she had not told anyone that she was receiving food stamps, so she could not figure out how Adam knew. Eve was puzzled, so she began to do some research. After making some calls, Eve discovered that Adam's aunt was a supervisor in that department. Eve also found out that her social worker and Adam's aunt were excellent friends, and they shared all her information with Adam.

Eve was so frustrated that she got a lawyer. Eve could not believe that she was being framed for fraud. Adam continued to harass Eve to stop her from doing everything she had worked so hard to accomplish. On Sunday night, around 10:30 pm, a police officer arrived at Eve's home and officially arrested her for food stamp fraud. Eve was enraged and could not believe what was happening. Everything inside Eve wanted her to hate Adam, but she tried her hardest to see the bright side. Eve was quickly bailed out of jail until she had to appear in court. Eve met a few times with her court-appointed lawyer, and she was confident that the lawyer would get to the bottom of everything. As the court date approached, Eve realized she judged the lawyer incorrectly because she did not investigate her case. She just looked at Eve as another case number she was trying to eliminate from her workload. The court date arrived, and Eve was very nervous, but she still held onto her faith in God. Eve often prayed so she knew the enemy was hot on her trail.

Eve entered the courtroom, and the judge asked her to place her right hand on the Bible and to repeat after him. "I will tell the whole truth and nothing but the truth, so help me God," the judge read as Eve repeated. The judge read the information from the case and asked Eve how did she plead to the allegations. Eve told the judge, "Not guilty." Eve's lawyer jumped up and whispered in her ear and told her if she pleaded "not guilty," they would have to go to trial, and if Eve were found "guilty" during the trial, they would give her guaranteed jail time. The lawyer then explained that if she pled "guilty" now, there would be no trial or jail time. Instead, Eve would receive a misdemeanor charge instead of a felony on her record. The lawyer was trying to convince Eve to plead "guilty" so she could close the case without working hard.

Eve felt invisible and unheard. She didn't know what to do because she knew they would not rule fair on her behalf. Eve even wanted to tell her story but was too afraid to lose and go to jail. She began to question God even more in her head. She wondered how she ended up in a situation where nobody cared about the truth, but during the opening remarks, they told her to give the truth. Tears fell from Eve's eyes as she looked around the courtroom because Eve knew she didn't have a fighting chance if she pleaded "not guilty." Eve thought of her children at that moment and did not want to go to jail. The judge asked Eve once more, "How do you plead?" With great humiliation and sorrow, Eve said, "guilty." That instant, embarrassment, shame, and rage overtook her. Eve also had to pay the state back the money she received in food stamps. That day Eve's life changed, and she built a wall never to trust anyone again. After court, Eve returned and held her sons because she was grateful to be with them instead of in jail. Eve hated being unable to tell her side of the story, but her boys were more important.

When it rained, it poured for Eve. It seemed like she could not get a break from her ex-husband's tricks and lies. A little while after the court situation, she received a call from Child Protective Services. The woman on the line said Adam called to make a complaint. The investigator said they went to the daycare to speak to the teacher, and she needed to visit the house to complete the investigation. That day the CPS worker met Eve at her apartment and asked her children different questions in the meeting. The worker quickly looked around Eve's place, then told Eve they would be back with results the next day. Before the CPS worker left, Eve asked for details about the complaint Adam had reported. The worker expressed that Adams complained about the boys grabbing their lower abdomen and saying their penis hurt. Eve was so over Adam's games that she began to laugh and proceeded to explain to the CPS worker. She told the social worker that she drives fast down the heel near their home because her boys love it. Eve also explained that she works in the medical field, so she teaches her boys the correct names of body parts. The CPS worker thanked Eve for the information and left the apartment. CPS got back to Eve the next day and informed her that they had dropped the complaint and closed Eve's case.

It took Eve months to settle herself mentally. She had to release worry and anxiety so it would no longer hold her down. Eve was coming around slowly, but she never stopped working towards healing. Every day was a process for Eve to forgive Adam for everything he did to her over time. From abusing her in every area of her life to trying to sabotage her name and character, Eve knew forgiveness was the right thing to do. Forgiveness is not for the abuser but for the victim to be free so God can come in and deal with the matter and the people involved. Forgiveness is the first step to healing. Eve wanted to be emotionally and mentally available for her children, so she had to let go of the hurt and past to move forward.

Eve had missed a lot of the bright side of life because of the traumatic experiences, so she fought to get back to that place. She wanted to live her life as a free woman again. Eve began to do things that made her happy and took her mind to beautiful places. She joined a production team and started acting in gospel plays. Eve loved every moment on stage because she could pour herself out to the people and be heard again. Eve knew acting was just what she needed to escape the dark place.

Several years have passed since Eve left Adam, and she is happier than ever. Eve has not remarried and has raised two handsome, intelligent boys soon to go off to start their own lives. Eve graduated nursing school in 2013 and even moved into a beautiful four-bedroom home. She now lives in peace and no longer looks over her shoulder for evil to break out. With God, all things are possible, even though they may appear to tarry. Wait on God, and He will show you the way.

CHAPTER 5

Angel Wings

Biblically, angels are heavenly beings commissioned by God for special jobs in heaven and earth. Their primary duty is to be intermediaries between God and man. The word angel comes from the Greek word "anggelos," meaning "messenger." Angels are usually identified with divine light, multiple eyes, bird wings, and warriors.

Angel wings symbolize the creative power of God and the way He covers and protects all His creation. God's angels are the purest expression of winged spirits, heavenly beings of God's love. It is one thing to read of angels or to see them in a book, but truly having an encounter with one will change your life forever. God has a chosen group of people that walk as angels who care, help, protect, love, and encourage others. Those selected for this type of work are not always aware of their mission.

Hebrews 13:2 NIV, "Do not forget to show hospitality to strangers, for by so doing some people have shown hospitality to angels without knowing it."

For many years I had a personal relationship with an angel and was utterly unaware. God already knew what my life would be like, what I'd need, and how it would turn out. Many times, we do not realize God's plans are not the plans we had for ourselves but greater. Allow me to explain.

On March 5, 1976, my guardian angel was born. Her name was Stephanie Lynn Hall. Stephanie means "crowned." From day one, she wore her crown. From a very early age, we became friends as far back as wearing diapers. We grew up together in the same neighborhood. Our parents lived within walking distance and were friends. Stephanie and I both had loving and supportive parents who were married. Our likes and dislikes were similar, except when it came to boys. We did not share the same attraction to the same types of boys, which made it easy for us not to like each other's boyfriends. I grew up as a "tomboy" who loved the outdoors and getting dirty. I could care less about my hair, and I did not wear jewelry. I loved jeans and sneakers but hated Sundays because I had to wear a dress with thick white tights. My mom even put shiny Mary Jane shoes on me and ribbons in my hair. Sometimes she would make me wear a shawl with my dress, and I could not stand it even more. I had a hard time trying to run and play in a dress and slippery shoes, although my mom did not want me outside on Sundays because she knew I would get dirty.

On the other hand, Stephanie was the "girly girl." She loved putting on dresses, jewelry, and shiny shoes. She loved her glamour shot attire. Stephanie even loved all the different hairstyles her mom did with bows and ribbons. Stephanie wore nail polish, lip gloss, etc., but I had difficulty keeping Vaseline or lotion on my face. Even with our differences, we had so many things in common. We accepted each other for who we were. Believe it or not, we were more alike than different. We were inseparable. People would mistake Stephanie's mom for being my mom because she had a light-skin complexion like me. They would even confuse Stephanie with being my mom's daughter because they were both brown-skinned. People would mix our moms up all the time, mainly because we all spent a lot of time together.

Stephanie and I went to parties and even family functions together. When you saw her, you saw me, and vice versa. We were best friends to the end and even considered each other sisters. As we got older, we even went on double and blind dates. You name it. We did everything together. I had her back, and she had mine. Stephanie would cover up for me when I told a lie, so I would not get into trouble. We would give each other a secret eye signal and always knew what the other was thinking.

In our 10th-grade year of high school, Stephanie was diagnosed with Multiple Sclerosis (M.S.). The disease affected and severely weakened her muscles. When her legs and lower body became too weak to move, she was permanently wheelchair-bound. I was so worried about her and thought she would die too young. I was not ready to lose her. She was my world, and I would not have known what to do without her by my side. I would regularly check on Stephanie, but she would always let me know she was okay. She would never complain or have a sad moment. Stephanie remained strong and positive. She was determined and ambitious to get her goals accomplished. I was encouraged to see her fighting through the pain and restrictions with ease. I considered Stephanie special because she went through so much at an early age but always smiled. She had every reason to become bitter and give up on life, but she chose greater and beat the odds. Even the wheelchair did not slow her down. She would get dressed, and her hair and nails would always be well put together. Stephanie even wore high heels. She did not allow the disease to slow her down.

People were always attracted to Stephanie because she was fun, outgoing, loving, and willing to help anyone and everyone. She inspired many who crossed her path. She was remarkable indeed. Stephanie even put together a support group for those affected by Multiple Sclerosis and their caregivers. She gave it her all because she wanted to bring awareness to the disease in hopes of having researchers pour more money into discovering a cure. Stephanie put together lesson plans, found a building, passed out flyers, and made announcements to different churches and community members to make sure the support group was a success.

Of course, I was there every step of the way to help Stephanie with anything she needed. The very first meeting was a success, and about 20 people joined. Stephanie continued holding the support groups until she could not attend because of multiple hospital visits. I stepped up to oversee a few of the meetings in her absence, but the group meetings soon ended because it was not the same without her. Everyone enjoyed the support group because it was very educational and a safe place to share emotions that no one else understood. God gave Stephanie that vision, and we give Him all the glory. God is so amazing! He orchestrated everything so well.

Over time, Stephanie got so sick that she spent much time in the hospital. I knew her day was coming soon, but I did not want to accept it. God began to show me dreams of myself standing in the gap to prepare for Stephanie's home-going. I would wake up screaming and crying many nights because I was not ready to let her go. Just the mere thought of her not being by my side was too much for me to bare. Stephanie stayed strong mentally, emotionally, physically, and spiritually. Half the time, she would tell the doctors how to treat her. I was used to Stephanie always recovering quickly, but this time even a simple bedsore was too much for her to fight off. The infection spread throughout her bloodstream. She began to stop eating and lost so much strength. I still had faith that she would recover as she always did. Stephanie would always look at me and say, "Stop worrying. I'm not going anywhere."

Stephanie told me that every day until December 1, 2014. That day I walked her to the bed, and she yelled loudly, "We gotta go!" I asked her, "Where are we going?" She looked at me and said, "You can't go!" I knew right then she was telling me goodbye. At that moment, my heart ripped out of my chest, and I began to pray. I began to scream and plead with the Lord to give me more time with my only friend, my best friend, and my sister. I begged Him not to take her away. Stephanie repeatedly said, "It's time to go, and you can't come." I did not know how to live without Stephanie because she was the strong one. I needed her to push me when I felt weak. At that moment, Stephanie's health started to decline fast. I will never forget that day.

Three days later December 4, 2014, I was trying to get some sleep when I could smell Stephanie's scent. The scent was so intense I jumped up and looked around because I thought she might have been standing by my bedside. There was no one there, so I laid back down. Then I smelled her scent again, even stronger! I felt alarmed, so I sat up in my bed and called out her name. I was not sure if it was her spirit that came to me to say her last goodbyes, but I felt her in my room. By faith, I began to speak into the atmosphere to let Stephanie know I received her goodbye and that I would miss her dearly. After I told her I loved her, the smell left my room, and within 15 to 20 minutes, my phone rang. Stephanie's sister-in-law was on watch duty that night with her. Before Stephanie's sister-in-law could say a word, I knew Stephanie was gone and the Lord had taken her away. I felt somewhat at peace because I could say goodbye, but I still had my breakdown moments.

Some say it gets easier with time, but it's been years, and it sure hasn't felt any easier to manage my emotions. I think of Stephanie every day. I even catch myself wanting to call Stephanie, then remember she is gone. I still feel like it's a dream that I haven't woken up to reality yet. I cannot wrap my mind around the fact that she is no longer here. All our memories seem like they were made just yesterday. I remember the many talks and laughs we shared, particularly in the backyard. No one would ever know what I went through the day I lost her because this is just a glimpse. I felt as if a piece of me died too. I did not want to live on, but I knew she would have wanted the best for me, and that was to live.

Every single day I miss my best friend. I am grateful for all the love she poured into me and everything she taught me. I am honored to have had the opportunity to spend many years with her. She will always be an angel to me, and I'm glad she has her angel wings now. Until I see her again, I will always hold tight to the memories we made together.

CHAPTER 6

Mercy & Grace

Mercy is defined as compassion or forgiveness shown toward someone whom it is within one's power to punish or harm them. God's mercy can never be explained. We aren't worth anything more than filthy rags, yet He shows us mercy daily. God's mercy keeps us safe from hurt, harm, and danger. It's His mercy that we can move, eat, walk, breathe, see, etc. Mercy is given to each of us every second of the day. Some of us don't even think about it, but not one of us deserves God's mercy. Kindness, humility, understanding, and love are some ways I define mercy. It is God's mercy that changes our hearts from stone to flesh. God's mercy expresses His perfect, unconditional love for us. God's mercy is extended to us where and when we need it the most because the Lord is merciful. He comforts His people and has compassion for those who are afflicted.

Isaiah 49:13, "Blessed are the merciful for they shall receive mercy."

Matthew 6:7, "His mercy is bigger than any of your mistakes."

Grace is defined as the free and unmerited favor of God, as manifested in the salvation of sinners and the bestowal of blessings. We experience many blessings in different ways—some we acknowledge, and others we don't even recognize. God is a loving father who blesses us even when we overlook them. He has priceless favor in store for us all. His grace is the strength that keeps us going when we feel like giving up. When our soul is down, our body is tired, or our minds feel overwhelmed, God's grace fine-tunes our dim light to shine bright again.

There was a time in my life when all I had was doubt, disappointment, and questions. I would ask God why things have turned out opposite from the norm in my life. Then I had to ask myself, what is the norm? People tend to categorize what is right and wrong according to social norms, but it is never what God intended. When God asks us to stand apart and follow Him, we fall apart. The church even uses religion to put the people in social norm boxes. Society wants to control our lives so that we become distracted and programmed as robots. Control is power, and it starts mentally. If society can control our minds, then they have power over us. Therefore, be set apart.

Let me give you an example. In the '70s, my parents wore afros. The average height of their hair was 6ins.-10ins. That was the norm because everyone followed each other. What about when you want to be different? There was a boy who dared to be different and wore a small afro instead of keeping it big like everyone else's. Everyone looked at him as if he was in sin. They laughed at him, mocked him, and pushed him away. Events like this happen all the time when someone wants to step outside of the social norm box. I can relate to receiving friction when I dared to be me in a trend-following world. We must realize God created us all differently, and it's okay to express those differences. During these times, it takes the strong leader in us all to stand for what we believe is right according to God's Will and Word. A lack of control can overtake us when we can't be who God created us to be, making us feel worthless, angry, and depressed. I pray we walk in the purpose God created for us instead of following the world's way. Jesus wants us to follow Him, so let's start today.

CHAPTER 7

Pure Love

What is pure love?

There are many forms of love, but the highest form is pure or agape. Pure love is God's unconditional love. It is not contaminated with selfish motives and an unclean heart. God's love gives freely, and it does not fail.

1 Corinthians 13:4-8 NIV, "Love is patient, love is kind. It does not envy, it does not boast, it is not proud. It does not dishonor others, it is not self-seeking, it is not easily angered, it keeps no record of wrongs. Love does not delight in evil but rejoices with the truth. It always protects, always trusts, always hopes, always perseveres. Love never fails. But where there are prophecies, they will cease; where there are tongues, they will be stilled; where there is knowledge, it will pass away."

1 Corinthians chapter 13 outlines the love of God. It is essential to live by this scripture so that we do not find ourselves in error and heartbroken. If we all lived as God intended, then the world would be a better place. When it comes to relationships and even marriage, it is imperative to give pure or true love according to God's definition. I have had my share of love outside of God's plan, and I did not like it one bit. It was selfish, greedy, prideful, abusive, and disrespectful love that I thought was good because it came with a smile, good sex, or even gifts. I am very selective now when it comes to love. If I don't receive the love of God, I do not want it. I believe most women pour out so much of themselves only to come up with

the short end of the stick! Therefore, I want to speak to the men that struggle with giving true love for just a bit in hopes that they would change for the better.

When it comes to true love, men, you must be open and honest with yourselves first to meet a woman's needs. Men, know what you want before you even seek a real woman that knows what she wants already. Weigh out the pros and cons. Are you ready for a lifetime partner? Or do you wish to have a good time for a moment? Do you want a "yes" woman who agrees with everything you say? Or do you want a woman with an opinion, education, backbone, and a willingness to stand up for herself and others? Do you want a woman willing to work hard for her family and respect her husband's hustle? Do you want a woman that has her husband's back through everything? Most women love hard, so be honest with your needs. There are levels to women, and we all should be clear about what we want out of someone. Men, when seeking a woman, ask yourselves these questions so there will not be any miscommunication. Let's face it. Men were born to seek women because the scripture, "He who FINDS a wife finds a good thing and finds favor with the Lord," tells us that man must find what God has placed on the earth just for him.

Women are built to love and care because we are nurturers at heart. We also crave love in return, hence why God commanded the husbands to love their wives as Christ loves the church. We all know Jesus died for us, so there should be the exact resemblance in marriage. Most women genuinely love simple things, but men that are confused with their needs will make everything complicated. Just a simple hug can do it for a woman. A hug could brighten up her whole day, but if the man is only focused on work or sex, he will miss it. Women pay attention to details where the man overlooks them to jump right to the big things. Sometimes this causes friction or miscommunication between the two. Men and women are not built the same, but if we can be honest and open vocally with each other, things could work in our favor.

Men must know their place for everything to run smoothly. Therefore, men cannot be confused. We all have a place, and knowing is only half the battle. God is always first, then man, then woman. If it is not in that order, it will not benefit anyone. I have experienced too much to accept anything outside God's will. I cannot and will not settle. God even instructed me not to settle but to wait on Him. He knows best and has the best for me. I must be patient. No longer will I give to the swine that do not value me, and I get nothing in return. No longer will I carry the weight of a man that's set for him to accept. Women were designed to be helpers, not enablers. Women can do it all, but that is not our place. She should not be burned out while her husband sits back and allow her to do his part along with her own. Love is also knowing your place and doing your part.

Submission is another conversation that is miscommunicated between men and women that do not have a Godly understanding of true love. To submit does not mean to bow down to another person physically. It's the posture of your heart. We must give up ourselves unconditionally by submitting our hearts to each other as we do to God. Therefore, we must have a relationship with God first. Men and women tend to get the wrong idea when it comes to submission because pride and selfishness creep in. A part of love is submission because we should do for others as if we were doing it for God. I touch on marriage throughout this chapter because it's the relationship that takes the most work. You cannot take shortcuts in marriage because it is the highest covenant in the earthly realm between two people. Marriage binds man and woman together to become one flesh, and pure love is critical to success. When you have a relationship between work partners, siblings, parent/ child, friends, etc., cracks in true love aren't really blown out of proportion. On the other hand, gaps in love are magnified in marriage, and when it fails, everything is out of order. Marriage is sacred to God, and He honors what He puts together. Therefore, let us all be mindful of giving pure love, even when it hurts, because love is also a sacrifice. Once men and women get on the same page, love should hurt less and become a beautiful story for someone else.

We still have much work to do. Not everyone knows the way of God, so there will be an imbalance in love at first. Most women tend to deal with more than they should because they feel they should hang in there. Women are supportive, and they don't want to give up until the job is complete. Most times, women give love and do not get it back in return. Women do not give up quickly once they give their all. When it comes to men, they do the complete opposite. They are built to be strong, take hits, and keep going. Men sometimes give up easily or move on to the next quickly. Often men would not show their inner emotions to a woman because it leaves them vulnerable, and they want to protect their ego.

A man's ego keeps them in pride and sometimes misses the woman set aside for them. Most men would rather walk away than work it out. Finding another woman sometimes is much easier for a man than dealing with all the damage they caused. Men even think sometimes the grass is greener on the other side, but that is not the case. The grass is only green where you put in the work. Men tend to run to another person's grass because it looks like it's less work, but when they get there, they discover it's sometimes artificial. Looks are not always what they seem. They say, "everything glitters isn't gold." Since men are more visual, they get fooled by the rich green grass that is actually plastic.

On the other hand, real women know that all grass takes work to get to the ideal expectation. Therefore, women are not afraid to roll up their sleeves to get dirty, or they would hire a landscaper to fertilize the grass if they are too busy. Women like to admire the beauty of their grass. Once a woman begins to do things independently without a man, she places a wall up, so there is no return. When a woman is done, she is done. So, men, I want to encourage you all to love genuinely and to know what you want out of life, especially when it comes to seeking after a woman. A scorned woman is not the side you ever want to see.

Pure love wants nothing in return. God's love is the purest and should be our example to follow. He does not measure His love nor love us according to emotion. His love is constant and truly genuine. God's divine love is selfless. God is love, and love is God. With love, anything is possible. Sometimes we have a hard time loving the way God does because of our past hurts and our inability to forgive at that moment. Also, loving ourselves is crucial. We must start there so we can properly love others. I remember putting myself on the back burner for many years. I even allowed people to take advantage of me. I lost myself in the process and forgot what I liked in life. My focus was wanting to be loved. I only got abuse in return, which is not love. I was yelled at, called out of my name, cheated on, etc., and I stayed thinking that love would grow, but it was never there in the first place to flourish. I had to get to a point where I knew my self-worth.

The Lord had to show me the true definition of pure love. He showed me how to love and how to give love. I now know what I will accept and what settling will do. I am a child of the Most High God. I am royalty because God is the King of kings, and I am His daughter. I am grateful to be adopted by Him and partake in His inheritance. He loves me and has loved me since the beginning of time. God's pure love helps me to be okay with waiting for someone else to come in and love me the same. Being lonely can sometimes cause us to rush into the arms of the wrong person.

Loneliness tells us that we should fear being alone. But if we have a relationship with God, we are never alone. Therefore, loneliness should never take over our minds. Being alone and lonely is two different things. No one knows me like God does because He created me, so He knows my ends and outs. I sit with Him in prayer so I can not only learn more about Him but learn more about myself as well. I have started dating myself. At first, I thought it was weird, but I had to let go of those thoughts and try them. I have realized certain things I like to do while spending time with myself that I didn't before. I did not know how much a bubble bath relaxed me and brought joy to my mind until I started exploring certain things to do alone. When I took the initiative to love and care for myself, I found freedom I did not realize was always there. I just had to tap into it. I have become okay and content with doing things alone. I know one day, God will send the partner that he has for me so that we can do things together, but in the meantime, I will not rush into anything.

Since I have been in a place where I am growing my relationship with God, He has shown me agape or unconditional love. That type of love is never changing but always abounds selflessly and purely. The Lord does for us daily and never throws it in our faces. I am so glad that His love never fails for us. God's love is so strong that it can be overwhelming at times, and our minds will never fully understand the measure of His love. I challenge you to try God and fall in love with Him for yourself.

Motherhood

I am a single mother of two very handsome boys I love dearly. I'm super proud of how far I've come with raising them. Through it all, I've been blessed. We all go through storms to strengthen our faith. Although motherhood has its ups and downs, being a mother is the most rewarding job in the world.

I refer to my children as gifts from God. A mother's love is powerful, however lasting, and pure. Mess with her children, and you will see a true sci-fi creature.

Women don't fully understand this type of love until they have children. God's love is in full operation from the moment we look into their eyes to admire what God has given us. There is nothing a mother won't do to protect her babies. I'm not talking about the two percent of women that drop the ball with parenting, but the ones that take on the responsibility seriously. Once I had children, I was very protective over them. If I was home, so were they. When I went out, they did too. I would not just allow anyone to watch them or be around them. I remember someone saying to me now that they are young, you keep them close, but that won't last long. Well, newsflash, they are now 18 and 21. I am the same way. My boys are my gifts, and I am all in when it comes to being their mom, especially since I had to go through much hell to bring them into the world. I value their lives. If you are a mother, you know what that type of love is, and to think Jesus loves us more than that is mind-blowing for me. For me, it's hard to imagine not loving them the way I do. Even during the night, if one of my boy's breathing changes, I wake up. I know when they are sleeping or awake. Mothers have strange senses when it comes to their children. I often sat and thought about how wonderful it is to be a mother. It is such an honor. God trusted me to be Shane and Caden's mom. That alone is enough to thank God forever.

When they were younger, I wanted them to slow down so I could get enough time with them. Before I know it, they will be gone to start their journey through adulthood. I love the summer because school doesn't separate our time together. I can see them every day, all day, in the summertime. We get to hang out and take trips to build memories. I even considered homeschooling them because we would spend even more time together. I'm sure some of you are saying this woman is totally crazy. Ha-ha. No, I'm not. I just love my boys and motherhood. I do not want to miss any moment that I can spend with them because I know when they get older, they will leave the nest and create their own families. As for now, I keep them close and covered with prayer. By God's grace, He keeps us all.

Daily we hear children go missing, killed, abused, on drugs, and raising themselves. When I hear these things, it hurts my heart. Why is this happening? It must stop! Pray for your children, anoint them with oil, and teach them God's love and the way they should go in God according to His Word. We are all responsible for our children, and we must remember that they belong to God first.

I can't give my children everything they want, but I make sure their needs are met. We raise our children differently, but we should all love them the same. Most times, we as mothers have the same desires for our children, which is for them to be healthy, happy, and prosperous, but it doesn't always work out that way. I'm praying for all moms and children alike. I pray all would have an understanding of Jesus and accept Him and also have an authentic relationship with God. I do not take away from the dads needing a relationship with God, but my story is to shine a light on the true love within single motherhood. I know I cannot be everywhere with my children to protect them, but the Lord is there to cover them in my absence, which gives me peace. The Lord loves us with everlasting love, and I am grateful to know His love.

CHAPTER 8

Faith

According to Hebrews 11:1 NIV, "Now faith is confidence in what we hope for and assurance about what we do not see."

Faith is trust, hope, and unfailing belief in God. God requires us to obey His commands, love Him with all our heart, mind, and soul, and have faith in Him. God's word tells us that if we have faith the size of a tiny mustard seed, we can move mountains, and miracles follow those that believe or have faith!

I remember seeing the people in the church living for God and walking in faith. I used to be amazed and wanted to be like them without being bored. I thought I would have to give up all the fun things I did to walk by faith. I knew I had to die to myself to follow Christ. I understood I could not do the things everyone else did in the world. The Holy Spirit must be able to move freely in me to change me. Doing what I want to do stops Him from moving because I enter the sinful nature of the world. I knew Jesus was the right choice, but I still wanted to do my own thing. I wasn't ready to live life according to God's commands.

I know so many people probably had these thoughts as well, but let me break it down for you so you can understand a little better. We cannot live a double life when it comes to serving God. His word tells us to be hot or cold but not lukewarm. God does not want someone who follows Him one day and the next day to disappear. We must make every effort to stick to God's commands outlined in His word. God wants us to love what He

Baptized in Tyler's Beach
by Pastor Leslie L. Halloway (right)
and Reverend Roberts (left)
October 09, 2020

loves and hate what He hates. God loves us but hates the sins we commit. If we want God to fight our battles, we must align with His will. We also must make sure we are connected to God through His son, Jesus.

The only way we can get to God is through Jesus Christ, accepting Him and giving up ourselves to follow Him. That is the only way we will make it into Heaven. I love the fact that God is very patient with us, and yes, we do have free will, but God's will is the only way to gain everlasting life. Every day our spirit and flesh are at war because our flesh wants the things that we were born into, such as the sin of the world that is against God's word. On the other hand, our spirit wants to connect with God and please Him. God does not force us to do anything. He sits back, watches, and waits for us to make up our mind. God is omnipresent; therefore, He is everywhere at once. So do not think that you are hiding anything from God. He sees everything, even the choices hidden in your heart.

Some believe there are three entities at work among us, but that is not true. There are only two at work. Either you align with God's word, or you have joined Satan's team by default. If you do not choose a side and think you are choosing yourself, or nothing, such as an atheist, you, too, have joined Satan's team by default. Even if you take your time with choosing God and have the understanding to make a sound choice, every moment you wait, you're working with Satan. We must make a conscious choice to choose the things of God. Outside of that, we are partnered with Satan. Now, some people purposely follow Satan by choice, and it would take a move of God to free them. Don't get me wrong, God still loves everyone because we are all His creation, even Satan, but it saddens Him when He is not our choice.

Even when we don't choose God the first time, He gives us opportunities to choose Him willingly, follow His ways, and love Him. God is patient with us. To love God is to obey His commands. Love is an action. Therefore, when we follow the ways of God and not just read them in the Bible, our actions show God that we love Him. Most of the time, we are stuck in our ways, and it takes something tragic to force us to turn to God.

Years ago, I thought I gave the Lord full access to my heart but discovered that I was not entirely devoted. God wants our whole heart, not just a little. In November 2014, when the doctor said my best friend only had weeks to live, it almost took me out. I was overwhelmed with emotions. I remember going home crying so hard that I lost control over my mind and body. I could barely walk or breathe, but I made it to my bedroom and fell across the bed. I started screaming at the top of my lungs, hoping to release some pressure from the news I had heard. I thought I could be strong for my best friend, but I couldn't wrap my mind around it all. I felt depression and suicide creeping into my room. My mind was too upside down to pray for myself or my best friend. My mind raced all over the place as tears drenched my pillow.

I thought to myself, "how could this happen to me?" Then it dawned on me that she was the one about to die, so I shouldn't be selfish. Why is this happening to us? I was so connected to her that I felt as if I was dying too! I needed her by my side. I soon came to the reality that I could not control death. That part was only a job for God. Trying to stand in the way of God's plan only revealed I didn't trust God and that I needed to do a better job. God has the final say in all things. Therefore, I asked God to forgive me and give me the strength to handle losing my only best friend. I was so drained from the stress. I wanted God to take me instead of her. God had to step in and take over at that moment because I was lost and at the point of giving up. I was hurting, and pain kept surging through my body and mind.

I could feel the stress breaking down my cells, muscles, and everything else within me. Stress is one quick way to die.

That night I finally got to a place of surrendering my emotions, thoughts, words, and actions to God. I begged Him to have His way with me. Immediately I could feel the Holy Spirit invade my room because I did not feel so alone. Yes, I still felt pain in my body from the stress that rushed through me, but I knew that my savior was there to lift the majority of the weight. God reminded me how much He loves me and that I had to continue life because it was not my time to go. We do not have the option to choose when we die because we all belong to God. He created us with a born date and a death date. I made up my mind and surrendered everything to God. Only the Lord could fight the battle I faced.

Right then, I gave myself to the Lord for real and wholeheartedly. That has been some years now. There is a significant difference between giving God a half "yes" and a full & sincere "yes." I used to worry about being bored or not having fun if I chose God's ways, but I know now that I need Him, so nothing else matters to me. Living for God is a sacrifice that I am now willing to make and have been making. It is a process, but I am learning every day.

The more the Lord shows me things, the more I want to learn. I have a thirst for the things of God that only the Lord could fill. Of course, I still go through bad times, but to have the Lord walk with me and help me handle life is better than doing it alone. Today I know without a shadow of a doubt that my relationship with the Lord is sincere. He has become my new best friend, husband, and anything else I need.

My relationship with God is open and honest, just as any other relationship I have had. When I'm upset, or He is upset at me, we release to each other and do what needs to be done to solve the problem. Sometimes He even nags me to do things until it's done. I know that He loves me, and I love Him. Until you take a chance with the Lord being your all, you will never fully understand my point of view. So, I challenge you to give it a chance. Start small by talking to the Lord in prayer and go on from there. Many ask me how I know when the Lord is around because they are amazed by our relationship. I would have them close their eyes and walk up to them. Even with your eyes closed, you can feel when someone or something is there. That is the same way with God. You can feel Him, although you cannot see Him, so do not be afraid to open up to God. I love that God doesn't seek perfect people because, the truth is, we are all messed up.

God only requires us to be willing and obedient servants, and He would do wonders through us. Another way to get to know God is to read His word. The scriptures in the Bible give us a lot of information on God's character, emotions, desires, heart, etc. The more you study His word, the more the Holy Spirit will unlock revelation so you can go deeper than the pages. God wants the best for us, so much so that He adopted us as His children. He wants us to be happy and prosperous, have hope, and have a future with an expected end that is bright. God wants to keep us safe from harm. God even loves when we speak to Him daily, which is considered prayer. Prayer is an intimate conversation we have with the Father where we commune with Him. In prayer, we give God our needs and even petition Him on others' behalf. Prayer is a two-way conversation because God talks back to us. He shares His heart and purpose with us in return. Our hearts should be so intertwined with the Father's that we do not second guess His voice. That takes consistency in prayer. When we show God appreciation and give Him time in prayer, it also grows our relationship with Him.

I have been dedicated to prayer and getting to know God's heart. As a result, my mind and perspective on life have changed drastically. I used to do many things, such as drinking, partying, randomly dating, etc., but once God stepped into my life, it changed forever. I do not regret the change because it was for my good. I did not understand then, but I do now. When I was caught up doing what I thought was fun, I was dying on the inside. The more we conform to the world, the further we are from God. God is the light that brings life; otherwise, we are dead until we choose correctly. Life is about making the correct choice to have everlasting life. Once I chose God, I felt free! I felt as if weights had been released from my body. I could not believe all that I was carrying daily but thinking I was enjoying life where I was.

God cleaned me up and healed me. He even gave me an understanding of true love. Therefore, I know how to give it to myself and others, as well as what to expect from others. Once we accept salvation, which is to confess Jesus is Lord, the son of God, and God raised Him from the dead on the 3rd day, we must live a life of daily repentance to be in the right standing with God. Repentance is to turn away from our daily sins and return to God by following His commands. God will then forgive us, and we can move forward with His will for our lives. We all make mistakes, and God already knew that would happen, so He sent His son Jesus to die for our sins. God is forgiving and extends mercy and grace to us. He also corrects us so we can be realigned with His will. Our heart posture should always be of repentance and God's love. The Holy Spirit will help us to mature in the ways of God. Just be open and willing to walk through the process.

Throughout my journey of getting to know God on a deeper level, I have seen several characteristics that He possesses. I know God has a sense of humor because He is hilarious sometimes with what He does and says to me. At times He could be bossy, gentle, loving, stubborn, and angry. I have discovered that God is also patient, and His ways and plans are not ours. He also works in His timing. God's word says He corrects those

He loves, and I thank God for loving me because He corrects me when I am out of alignment. God also blesses us when we are obedient. You, too, could learn so much about God. Just continue to pray if you do pray, but if you don't, please start to pray. Also, get a Bible and begin to read. God's Holy Spirit will help you to understand. The goal is to start somewhere, and then God will help you to elevate your relationship with Him and become familiar with His purpose for your life. Once you start your journey with God, many will not understand, but that is okay. Just allow the Spirit of God to guide you. Your faith will only grow when you hear the word of God.

Therefore, continue to remain in His word. Have patience while you wait to hear from Him because sometimes, He does not answer right away. The Lord truly loves us, so always remember that while going through life changes. Walk your own pace with God because He will always meet you where you are. Just be open and honest with the Lord in every area of your life, and He will save and deliver you when needed.

Keep faith in God and trust Him with all your heart. The Lord always keeps His promise and His word because He is not a man that He shall lie. Remember, Satan works just as hard to keep you set back with him, so learn how to discern or distinguish between who is pulling on you. When you know that Satan is after you, allowing God to fight your battles will be a relief. I have been through too much not to have faith in God, and I have come too far to return to my old ways. God has been fighting for me for many years, and I am grateful to be on His team. He wins every time. Satan is no match for God. I will continue to live for God and follow His commands. I challenge you all today to start or to go deeper in your relationship with God because tomorrow isn't promised to anyone. Life is but a vapor.

CHAPTER 9
This Battle Is Not Mine

The word of God tells us the battles we face are not ours, but it belongs to the Lord. Once we fully mature in the word of God, we will understand why we must allow the Lord to fight our battles. Our troubles aren't meant to break us. They are intended to strengthen our faith. God gives us biblical stories to read, but until we experience these tests and invest sweat, blood, and tears, our prayers and faith will not elevate.

When we go through a situation, it's always best to have the Lord on our side because He shields us from turbulence. The Lord has our best interests at heart because He unconditionally loves the creation He created, which are you and me. A lot of us go through things and ask God why they had to happen to us, but my question is, why not you? When we are chosen, God has already equipped us to handle warfare and anything else that comes our way. Those chosen by God deal with a certain elevation of storms so that God can put them on display and get the glory out of their lives. If we were not stretched in areas where we are comfortable, we would not experience God's strength or realize His hand is upon us.

Sometimes we go through different trials and tests because we must reach unbelievers. We must be able to relate to them and not miss them as we minister to them. I often see "church people" act as if they are better than the "outsiders." I ask, "what are outsiders?" We are all children of God, and all of us fall short. Therefore, no one is better than the next. Some people have put themselves on a pedestal and think they are above others. They are the ones who cannot relate to or help someone who doesn't look, dress, or talk like them. That type of behavior or attitude will not get you into heaven either because it's all related to pride which got Satan kicked out of heaven. Surely, we will not make it there with pride! I have seen pride destroy churches, families, work environments, etc. When we have pride, it marks us with a stain and sets us apart from doing the work of the Lord.

Some churches are the breeding grounds for pride, where the people control and run the show to bring themselves glory instead of God. We should gather in churches to get to know God better and get trained to inform others. Everything should glorify God as His purpose is fulfilled. Instead, pride has the people genuinely there for God turn away from the church. We must remember only those things we do for Christ will last.

Also, I often see churches have the same people doing the same routine every time they gather, which gets tedious. The root of most of it is also pride because the leader, chairperson, or person in charge thinks they are the only ones that can fulfill the purpose of the task. Please do not misunderstand what I'm saying. Yes, certain people are called to specific things, and not everyone can do the job. Some in charge know there is help in the room and still do not welcome the assistance. Ministry is not meant to be done alone because there is much to do. Pride has made most churches a "one-man" show. Pride drives us to seek praise and applause, so they do not want to share the spotlight.

I want to remind you all that none of us are entitled to the spotlight because it all belongs to God. I even witnessed people call the church their own, but the church building should be God's house where all His children and those that want to learn about Him could come together. I see all the time that the order of the church is not God first, then the pastor, then the sheep, but it's the pastor, and that's all. Take a moment to sit and examine the church you attend. If God is not the head, I would suggest you run! Since God is not running the church, then it's Satan. Remember, it is God or Satan, no in-between. Destruction always comes after pride.

As our faith grows in God, we become more comfortable with being set apart or standing alone. It's called living holy and righteous according to God's standards. I'm not saying we should mature in God and forget everyone else, but when you know better, you do better, even if those around you are not. Those among us should also strive to elevate and do better, but if they are not, that connection should be cut. Those people will take us back to where we have come from if we are not strong enough. We should pull people to Christ, not allow them to pull us back into darkness. Some stubborn people know better but choose not to do better because they want to do their own thing.

As I expressed before, either we work for God or work for Satan. Therefore, when I see people that choose to work for Satan, I walk away and allow God to get them to the place they need to be in His timing. Our lives depend on us following Jesus Christ, not following others. Therefore, dare to be different and set apart. Do not compare yourself to others because you don't know the secret battles they face or if they are in the right standing with God. Allow God to lead you to the place that He created for you.

Remember, "What's for you is for you, and what's for them is for them." We need to get serious about doing God's will. In actuality, that is why we were all created. Do not allow people or yourself to lead you astray from the perfect will of God. Get to know God for yourself through prayer, fasting, and reading the Bible. Those things will help increase our knowledge and faith in God, and He will take over to do the rest. Be intentional about your relationship with God. We are intentional with everything and everyone else, but why not God?

Do not open your Bible only when you go to church on Sunday. It would help if you opened it to read a little every day. The pastor should not have to give you everything you need to know concerning the word of God. We must study God's word for ourselves as well. The great thing is we have the Holy Spirit to teach us God, one-on-one. We must be open to Him. There are even sermons on the internet that God will lead us to receive a deeper understanding. The Holy Spirit will also reveal revelation to us in the time that it's needed. The more time you spend seeking God, the more you will grow spiritually.

God loves us and desires a relationship that continuously runs deeper every day. His love for us is beyond anything that our minds could even comprehend. I urge you today to gain a better understanding of God and allow Him to elevate your faith. Once we fully trust God, we will know He has already worked our battles out.

CHAPTER 10

Growing Pains: Life Lessons

Growth is developing or maturing physically, mentally, or spiritually. It's also the process of increasing in amount, value, or importance.

Life lessons are obstacles we go through naturally in life that we learn from over time. These lessons push us to grow. God desires to take us to a new level once we accomplish the current one. He doesn't want us stuck in one place too long because we get complacent. The Bible says we should go from faith to faith and glory to glory, which means we should always be on the move. Each level is a test, and it can be complicated and a struggle, but God is with us. When we follow Jesus Christ, opposition will always be attached to deter or distract us from the goal of elevation. Once we go through the storm, God will always bring us out stronger and wiser. You will see life from a new perspective.

Losing my dad on September 3, 2022, completely changed my outlook on life. Before he passed, I thought I was strong and had everything figured out. I was not prepared to face a test as such. I was caught off guard and grew angry with God. Not that I thought we would be on earth forever, but I at least needed a warning. He gave me nothing! I know God does whatever He wants because He is in control of everything. I just

thought our relationship was deeper than the surprise death of my dad. Maybe He thought I would not take it well either way. I guess this fast, sharp cut was the best way. I pray God forgives me for being angry because I am really trying not to be but be understanding. I loved my dad beyond words and never imagined living without him. I was daddy's girl and connected with him when no one else understood me. When he passed, I felt alone, hurt, depressed, and unprotected. I could not understand why God would put me in such a situation. I thought I had more time with my dad. Now, I sit daily, trying to pick up the pieces of my life and attempt to move forward, only to get stuck every step I take.

I told you opposition will always come to distract us as we walk through the test, storm, or even the valley of death. Yes, I feel like a part of me died with my dad. I try to look for the good in everything and keep my faith, but it's harder said than done. I know God is with me, and He desires to heal me from this chapter of my life, but I don't know how to let Him in now that I am grieving and confused. He does all things for our good. I must remember that as I lay in my bed crying at night, thinking about my dad. I need God to continue to work on me and keep me from going insane. I know He wants to deliver me from this warfare, so I do not live here too long in my mind. I just have to surrender this battle to Him. That is the only way. There is a fight in my mind, and I do not know how to let go of this one yet. God might have to snatch it out of my hand. I have faced the death of a loved one before, so this should've been a little easier to deal with, but it's not. I need a little more time to adjust and process everything. Yes, my dad is in a better place, and we all must go, but his death was sudden. My dad's death almost took me with him. It tore through my world like a tornado came through, and nothing was left behind.

I have never experienced life without my dad around. I was fortunate enough to be raised in a two-parent household, and I was always welcome to visit home even after I moved out. My dad and I didn't start with the best relationship because he worked so much when I was younger, but over time we grew inseparable. My dad was my foundation and made me feel safe. He gave me advice and helped me when I needed it the most. With my dad gone, I have no one else to turn to because my family is struggling too. I thought they would have been there for me as I processed the loss of my dad, but that was not the case. I was surprised at some of them because I gave so much, only for them to turn their back on me. You know they say your family is the first to abuse you. They are the first in line to try to take you out. They reject and abandon you for dead, but I did not believe that until I looked around and had no one by my side. God requires us to love even when others do not do their part. Therefore, loving them is what I will continue to do.

"In the spring grove, I gave you all that I had for many years faithfully. I was there when you called. I did it all for you. No problem because of love. But when the tables were turned, and I needed you, where were you for me?" -Tiffany

The short end of the stick has been my portion outside of my dad, but now he is gone. I'm tired of giving my all because I don't get the same in return. I observe people because I like to learn their likes and dislikes. I listen to people and pay close attention to their needs. I enjoy helping others, but I have yet to have others go out of their way for me. I will keep the hope that God is preparing someone for me and use wisdom to know when to close my hand from now on. Once my dad passed away, I saw he was the only one that cared that much about me. I will miss him dearly.

I pray God keeps me moving forward through this process even when I want to give up. I know nothing happens by accident, and God still heals and is in control because He is sovereign. My deliverance is all in my surrender to Him. This test is designed to take me closer to God. Every day we should strive to go deeper with God because He will reveal more to us. I told God a long time ago that I wanted more of Him, but I did not know the price. Every relationship will cost you something. The difference with God is that when He takes people, places, and things away, He always gives bigger and better. Of course, nothing will replace my dad, but God wants to take over that void within me to become my Father. On that note, God is bigger and better than anyone in the world. Therefore, I am grateful to be His. God does whatever it takes to get our attention. He is a jealous God and does not want anyone taking His place. In many ways, I can see where I had my dad in the position where God desired to be. My dad did a great job, but God wants to supersede anything I have ever seen.

I am almost on the other side of wrapping my mind around it all. God has plans for me, and I know they are mind-blowing because of all the things I have had to endure in my life. God wants another "Yes" from me, and I will give it to Him. God desires to be our everything. The purpose of pain is to push us to persevere in the promises of God. Pain is not to cripple us but to keep us close to God. The way we perceive a thing is how we will go through it. Stay positive and speak life even through the storm. Pain is only temporary. You will make it if you faint not. Continue to pray, fast, and read the word of God because elevation, obstacles, and pain will be all our portion at some point in our journey. The Bible says there comes a time for everything. Therefore, stay connected to God. That is the only way we will make it through the trials. We are nothing without Him. Therefore, hold onto Him.

My dad used to say, "Listen to learn the word, learn to love the word, and love to live the word."

www.ingramcontent.com/pod-product-compliance
Lightning Source LLC
Chambersburg PA
CBHW051548120626
46551CB00013B/1420